MW00710270

Promotion of Social Righteousness

Cynthia L. Rigby

PRESS

Louisville, Kentucky

Publisher: Joseph D. Small

Editor: Mark D. Hinds

Writer: Cynthia L. Rigby

Book interior and cover design by Jeanne Williams

Published by Witherspoon Press, a ministry of the General Assembly Mission Council, Presbyterian Church (U.S.A.), 100 Witherspoon St., Louisville, Kentucky.

Unless otherwise indicated, Scripture quotations in this publication are from the New Revised Standard Version (NRSV) of the Bible, copyright © 1989 by the Division of Christian Education of the National Council of the Churches of Christ in the U.S.A. Used by permission. Every effort has been made to trace copyrights on the materials included in this book. If any copyright material has nevertheless been included without permission and due acknowledgment, proper credit will be inserted in future printings after notice has been received.

© 2010 Witherspoon Press, Presbyterian Church (U.S.A.), Louisville, KY. All rights reserved. No part of this book may be reproduced without the publisher's permission.

pcusa.org/witherspoon

PRINTED IN THE UNITED STATES OF AMERICA

*This book is dedicated to my husband,
William Greenway, the most faithful and
unfailing promoter of social righteousness I know.*

Contents

It is precisely in waiting for His appearing that we shall "be zealous unto good works." That the sober, righteous and godly life in this world is our life in *faith* is decided by the fact that it is a waiting for the epiphany of Jesus Christ.

—Karl Barth

Righteousness exalts a nation,
    but sin condemns any people.
        —Proverbs 14:34 (TNIV)

Introduction

When I was in college, back in the mid-1980s, I had the habit of taking long walks in a local park as a study break. Zealous for both changing the world and sharing my Christian faith (two callings that, I believed, were inextricably intertwined), I enjoyed having chance conversations with others who also had the time and inclination to talk.

One day I met an almost-elderly man who was cynical about life and clearly annoyed by my buoyant outlook. In the course of our conversation it became clear that he was even more eager to precipitate a change in me than I was to offer healing to him. Gaining no ground, he finally resorted to his own version of a prophetic word.

"By the time you're forty you'll see things more the way I see them," he said. "Your optimism about what 'God' is doing and how we can transform the world will be long gone."

"I'll tell you what," I said, frustrated and stubborn, "give me your address and I'll send you a postcard. I'll send you a postcard on my fortieth birthday to tell you I *haven't* changed about this. That *I still believe in God* and *us.*"

"But it won't work to send me a postcard," he pointed out, with the firm and steady tone of one who knows he is right on the cusp of victory. "It won't work because I'll already be dead."

Would I, in good faith, have been able to send that postcard on my fortieth birthday? Here I am, past that age, writing this book, and that man's words are still with me. They are—I must admit—truer than I once imagined they ever would be. On many days it is tough enough to survive the world, never mind making headway toward transforming it. I mean this on a personal level, and also on a corporate one. I write these words on a day in which the economic recession is deepening, and many of us are wondering just how much optimism about the future it is shrewd to maintain. We don't much want to look like that young woman of twenty-five years ago: walking in the park, annoying those we encounter with our naïveté about life, with its pain and complexities. Frankly, we're way too old for that.

And yet we, who are older than I was on that day in the park, still want to be vehicles of transformation in this world, don't we? After all, we are writing and reading this book for some reason. And—even more significantly—we continue to pray, as Jesus taught us: "Thy kingdom come! Thy will be done." We might pray this prayer with more or less gusto, depending on our circumstances. But, even after two millennia of praying, we still haven't given up.

This is a book about not giving up. It is a book that insists we become who we really are as members of Christ's body. The goal of this book is to envision how we—the church—might live, worship, and work as those who actively participate in bringing God's creative and redemptive will to fruition. It is about living into our identity as promoters of social righteousness, as the fifth Great End of the Church describes it.

This is a tricky subject, I admit. On one hand, it is all too easy to take on the mantle of responsibility for this Great End, as if we—as members of Christ's body—are somehow automatically "more righteous" than others. On the other hand, it is just as easy to run in fear of taking on the responsibility of promoting righteousness, concerned that we might be labeled know-it-alls. At certain times of my life, I have sat self-righteously on the proverbial "high horse," spouting off about how corrupt our society is, how the church is at least as bad, and how we really need to get our moral act together. And, at other times, I have shirked my prophetic calling in the name of being tolerant, open-minded, humble, and/or respectful of the differing views of others.

One thing I am certain of, and that I hope is reflected in this book: the promotion of social righteousness is neither about moral one-upmanship nor about being so open-minded that our brains fall out. I try, in these pages, to articulate a faithful alternative to these extreme options.

This book explores the concept of the promotion of social righteousness as a way of understanding ourselves in relation to the world in which we live. Though it is labeled an "end" of the church, the promotion of social righteousness is not appropriately understood as an enterprise that can be objectively evaluated, tackled, and accomplished apart from our own transformation into new creatures (see 2 Corinthians 5:17). In other words, it is not the case that the church is called to go forward and promote social righteousness as though fulfilling one of six responsibilities delineated in a job description. The promotion of social righteousness is not, first and foremost, about what we are called to *do,* but about who we are called to *be,* as the body of Jesus Christ. Therefore, it must be considered from the inside out—always in relation to who we are, as subjects who participate in the life and work of God, in and through the person of Jesus Christ, by the power of the Spirit.

Surveying the Landscape: The *Case* for Social Righteousness

This chapter serves to prepare readers for the journey into better understanding who we are as promoters of social righteousness. First, it identifies our starting point, explaining the relationship of this book to the Great Ends of the Church series as a whole. Second, it "packs our bags" for the journey by offering a historical overview: Where did this concept of promoting social righteousness come from, anyway? Third, it peruses our maps for the journey, highlighting the framing biblical texts and introducing a chart that gives an overview of the book's argument. With bags and maps at the ready, we move on, in chapters 2–4, to the heart of the matter: What does the promotion of social righteousness have to tell us about who we already are, and who we are called to be?

Our Starting Point: This Book's Placement in the Series

This book is the fifth of six in a series on the Great Ends of the Church. As listed in the *Book of Order* of the Presbyterian Church (U.S.A.), these ends are:

> the proclamation of the gospel for the salvation of humankind;
> the shelter, nurture, and spiritual fellowship of the children of God;
> the maintenance of divine worship;
> the preservation of the truth;
> the promotion of social righteousness; and
> the exhibition of the Kingdom of Heaven to the world.[1]

The series as a whole is committed to assisting the people of God in reflecting on what it means to be church. Not surprisingly, there is a good deal of overlap in the consideration of the particular ends. For example, the argument presented here presumes that the promotion of social righteousness is part and parcel of the proclamation of the gospel for salvation, since the good news is concerned with bodies, as well as with souls. It also understands, for example, that the promotion of social righteousness is one way the church exhibits the kingdom of heaven to the world. Keeping in mind that the starting point of our journey is the whole of what the church is (including all of its "ends") will guard us against reducing the purpose of the church to the promotion of social righteousness. To uphold any of the Great Ends at the expense of the others would be to misunderstand what it is to be church.

Packing Our Bags: The Promotion of Social Righteousness in Context

Its Meaning Then and Now

The concept of the promotion of social righteousness will not resonate immediately with many contemporary readers. One reason is because it is not a term used as commonly these days as it was during the Progressive Era (ca. 1890–1913). Christian believers today tend to understand themselves as either enduring an ungodly culture (neither *in* the world nor *of* it) or living in barely distinguishable relationship to the world (both *in* the world and *of* it). Those who see themselves as enduring might, at first glance, understand the promotion of social righteousness to be ultimately futile.[2] The second group might have the impression that promoting social righteousness is presumptuous. "Who am I to tell others what is right to do?" Presbyterians (among others) might reasonably ask themselves. Christian believers involved in the Social Gospel movement at the turn of the twentieth century perceived themselves as being *in* the world, but not *of* it. Their conviction was that teaching and living according to the mandates of the gospel would lead to the transformation of the society in which they lived. Christian believers who participated in the temperance movements, suffrage movements, and antislavery movements generally understood themselves to have a sanctifying role in relationship to the culture at large.

A popular manifestation of the turn-of-the-century commitment to the promotion of social righteousness is Charles Sheldon's 1896 novel,

In His Steps. The book had been translated into nearly two dozen languages by 1935 and was claimed by Walter Rauschenbusch, a leader in the Social Gospel movement, as the inspiration for his work. Some sources report that it is one of the top ten bestselling books of all time.[3]

In Sheldon's story, a pastor named Maxwell is challenged by a homeless man to live in light of his Christian convictions. This pastor, in turn, exhorts the members of his congregation to ask themselves, before every decision, "What would Jesus do?" As church members begin to take action in ways consistent with their answers to this question, the community surrounding the church is transformed. While the contemporary WWJD? movement (popular in the United States in the 1990s) tends to emphasize *individual* spiritual growth and renewal, the Social Gospel movement of a century ago, represented by Sheldon's story, focused on the renewal of *society*. The WWJD? movement of today addresses personal sin and is ardently embraced by political conservatives. In contrast, the politically liberal Sheldon was devoted to renouncing systemic, corporate sin. Optimistic about the capacity of human beings to change the world, he inspired action on the part of social progressives and was considered a socialist by some.

Just as WWJD? is commonly associated with theological and political persuasions very different from those of Charles Sheldon, those who currently encourage the promotion of social righteousness have a different agenda than our forbears who included the phrase in the Great Ends of the Church. An Internet search promptly reveals numerous essays and other contemporary materials associating the promotion of social righteousness with the support of "family values," the rejection of homosexual unions, the enforcement of severe means of discipline (including capital punishment), and the denial of abortion except in cases that threaten the mother's life. Those most commonly associated with the phrase in the early twentieth century would probably have taken different stands on some of these controversial issues than those who commonly claim the phrase today. They were engaged in a variety of social issues: They worked to remedy the dehumanizing impact of the slave trade; they advocated for women's suffrage; they fought for the basic rights of the worker. They believed that drinking alcohol was vile and immoral because it led to domestic violence, loss of employment, child neglect, unhealthiness, and poverty. All in all, those who upheld social righteousness were convinced that Christian believers can and should take political actions that advance the coming of the kingdom of God to earth as it is in heaven.[4]

To this point, we have tried to get a historical "feel" for what was and is meant by the concept of promoting social righteousness. I offer now a brief history of how scholars believe this end came to be adopted by the Presbyterian Church (U.S.A.).

Adoption by the Presbyterian Church[5]

The Great Ends of the Church, as they appear in the Presbyterian Church (U.S.A.)'s *Book of Order,* were shaped amid the same cultural currents Charles Sheldon navigated at the turn of the twentieth century. While the precise inspiration and authorship of the statement has apparently been lost,[6] we know it was first adopted in 1910 by one of the PC(USA)'s predecessor denominations, the United Presbyterian Church of North America (UPCNA).[7] Worthy of note, and another clue to understanding the character of the relationship between church and society in that time: This acceptance took place just two years after the Federal Council of Churches in the United States adopted the Social Creed of the Churches in 1908 (Appendix A).

The Great Ends of the Church came to be in the current *Book of Order* through two successive mergers of Presbyterian denominations culminating in the creation of the Presbyterian Church (U.S.A.) in 1983.[8] Attempting to trace the story of the Great Ends' adoption, Jack B. Rogers looks at the character of still earlier ancestors of Presbyterianism in America, the UPCNA's precursor denominations. Rogers says these denominations were made up of Scottish Presbyterian settlers who valued Scripture and the *Westminster Confession of Faith.* Rogers offers an interesting description of these early promoters of social righteousness:

> We think of [them] as a conservative component of our heritage. It is true that they practiced closed communion. They retained the Scottish free church practice of public covenanting to make their position known on moral issues. They were for the exclusive singing of Psalms in worship, without instrumental accompaniment. And they refused church membership to members of secret societies that required the taking of oaths.[9]

While they were conservative in relation to some church practices, Rogers insists that the UPCNA and its predecessors were surprisingly progressive in other ways. For example, the Associate Synod in 1811 declared the holding of slaves a moral evil, calling upon church members to free their slaves. The other predecessor denomination of the UPCNA—the Associate Reformed Church—declared in 1853 that *all* communing members could vote for pastors. This included women, who had been denied such voting privileges.

Referencing the work of William F. Keesecker (elected moderator of the UPCNA in 1975), Rogers suggests that the *Westminster Confession of Faith* and the *Larger* and *Shorter Catechisms* were the seeds of the Great Ends, which the UPCNA adopted without controversy as part of the revision of the church's *Book of Government and Directory for Worship*. Rogers writes, "The truths contained therein and their emphases were apparently characteristic of this Christian community."[10] He concludes,

> The United Presbyterian Church broadened and deepened those earlier definitions [from their predecessors] of the purpose of the church. In the context of its commitment to both the truth of God and forbearance in love, it developed a concept of the church that balanced conviction and civility. It included a balance of biblical emphases on evangelism and nurture, worship and truth, social action and the manifestation of holiness.[11]

Thus, the UPCNA seems to have been a Christian community that valued both personal and public morality.

Robert E. Blade notes that a reading of more than fifty years of General Assembly minutes of the UPCNA does not reveal any mention of the Great Ends. He writes: "Their formulation seems to have been a literary statement officially endorsed and forgotten."[12] However, careful study of these minutes is rewarded with deepened insight into the character of the church community in which the Great Ends statement was authored.

After studying the 1910 *Minutes of the Fifty-Second General Assembly of the United Presbyterian Church of North America,* Laura Elly Hudson reports on what seems to serve as evidence for the church's concern for social righteousness:[13]

- The "Report on Reform" notes that "the Decalogue is still in force and God has founded thereon His three-fold institutions of family, Church and State."[14] Recommendations on temperance and on the keeping of the Sabbath were offered. The suggestion was made that the church ought to encourage public legislation to strengthen Sabbath observance.

- The minutes reveal that the UPCNA was involved in both foreign and home missions. The church was also invested in what it called "Freedmen's Missions," educating and working with African Americans in many ways. One committee report expresses a protest against persecution of Jewish Russian immigrants, though it also intones that the need to evangelize the Jews is dire if the spread of Judaism is to be contained.[15]

- A quote from the "Report on State of Religion" seems indicative of the understanding of the word *righteousness* within the denomination: "That the religious life in the denomination is vigorous is further evidenced by the activity of our membership in the reform movements which make for the 'righteousness that exalteth a nation,' and which operate for the betterment of social and industrial conditions."[16]

- An example of the work for the "betterment of social conditions" comes from the "Report on Present Industrial Conditions." It suggests that in employment conditions there was a widespread antagonism between the laboring classes and their employers and that "present industrial conditions open up such a great field for Christian effort in securing for the laborer a more equitable share in the reward of industry; safer and more sanitary conditions of employment; the protection of women and children from the hard conditions of industrial life; the making clear to the employer the Christian obligations of sympathy and brotherhood . . . [and the] securing for both the blessings of Sabbath rest."[17]

These observations reflect the social and moral concerns of the era in which the Great Ends were written, helping us understand something of how the unknown authors of these ends understood the promotion of social righteousness. In short, the UPCNA was theologically conservative *and* socially progressive, upholding rigorous standards for personal morality and for the church's leading involvement in the public work of remedying social concerns.[18]

An informative and lively article by Gene TeSelle of the Witherspoon Society describes the history of the Social Creed's development and compares the conditions in which it was written with the conditions of our time.[19] This article was precipitated by the PC(USA)'s recent adoption of A Social Creed for the 21st Century (Appendix B), written by the National Council of Churches in 2008, the one-hundredth anniversary of the first social creed.[20] One of TeSelle's insights affirms the very purpose of our ensuing journey: "General Assemblies of the Presbyterian Church in the U.S.A. responded to [the early twentieth-century] 'social awakening' several times, adopting rewritten versions of the Social Creed and, *in typical Presbyterian fashion, adding biblical and theological backing."*[21] There is a real sense in which the enterprise of this book is to reflect on the biblical and theological backing for the promotion of social righteousness, respecting that which the Presbyterian Church (U.S.A.) has always understood to be essential to the Christian faith.

Now that we have said something about how the promotion of social righteousness was understood a century ago and how the concept came to be embraced by the Presbyterian Church, we are ready to turn more directly toward what it has to say about ourselves, and our vocation, as the body of Christ. As we step into this exploration, what biblical and theological "maps" do we have in hand to guide our way?

Our Maps: Aims and Argument of the Book

While in the course of our journey various passages from Scripture are referenced, three texts especially come into play.

Matthew 6:9–13[22]

This text, known to Christian believers through the ages as the Lord's Prayer, serves as scaffolding for this book's argument. As indicated in Figure 1 (p. 10), each of the next three chapters of this book is inspired by a line of this prayer: "Thy kingdom come!" (Chapter 2), "Thy will be done" (Chapter 3), and "On earth as it is in heaven" (Chapter 4). It is often noted that the Lord's Prayer is eschatological in nature, looking forward to the coming of the kingdom of God.[23] However, what is too often missed is that the prayer reflects deep commitment to and yearning for social righteousness as part and parcel of the coming of that kingdom.[24] To know God as "Father" is to yearn for God's promised kingdom, marked by the grace and love of which we have tasted (Chapter 2). To watch for the kingdom is to imagine what God desires, which in turn prepares us to participate in God's will as doers of justice, lovers of kindness, and humble walkers with God (Chapter 3). When we imagine God's will and begin to live into God's creative and redemptive intentions, we make manifest concrete signs of God's kingdom on earth. Where social righteousness is promoted, bread is eaten, human beings forgive each other, and the children of God are delivered from evil (Chapter 4).

Micah 6:8

"What does the Lord require of you?" the verse asks. The response delineates three things: (1) "to do justice," (2) "to love mercy" (TNIV), and (3) "to walk humbly with your God." While Micah 6:8 in one sense reads as though we are being let off easy (after all, it doesn't launch into lengthy, detailed directions about what we can and cannot eat, or how to go about honoring the Sabbath), anyone who is attentive to the three imperatives recognizes they are challenging to fully realize in practice.[25] In Chapter 3, I use these three "requirements" to frame the discussion, arguing that they help us to *imagine* what the kingdom of God looks like and, therefore, to begin participating in the concrete work of the kingdom.

Proverbs 14:34

A third text plays in the background of this work, a verse that seems historically to have influenced the development of this Great End. "Righteousness exalts a nation," we are instructed, "but sin condemns any people" (TNIV). This text seems to make one of the most direct references to social righteousness in the biblical witness. But whose is the righteousness of which this verse speaks, what is its character, and how does it exalt a nation? Chapter 2 of this book will argue that it can be only God's righteousness, and not our own, that exalts us. Chapter 3 will consider righteousness as it is manifested in the lives of the faithful, and Chapter 4 will consider what a righteous society might look like.

Figure 1 summarizes the argument as a whole. While readers with certain learning styles will appreciate seeing the chart at the start of the book, others might find it understandable only after they have read through the chapters (and, for this reason, might want to skip to Chapter 2). I hope that the interconnectedness of the chapters will become clearer as the book unfolds, and that offering this chart will help readers get a sense of the whole, at whatever point they choose to use it.

The chart offers an overview of the elements of the chapters. The downward arrows indicate that society's righteousness (Chapter 4) is the fruit of our righteousness (Chapter 3) as it is grounded in God's righteousness (Chapter 2). In talking about *our* righteousness leading to *society's* righteousness, the word *our* refers to the human beings created in the image of God to live as God's children. For the purposes of this book and its intended audience, I am primarily referring to self-identified members of Christ's church with my use of the term *our.* By *society's righteousness,* I refer to the infrastructure, systems, and institutions that manifest the righteousness being promoted by the children of God.

Notice how the three framing biblical passages I have mentioned are in play. Proverbs 14:34 provokes three major questions:

1. *Whose* righteousness exalts a nation?
2. *What* is righteousness?
3. *How* does righteousness exalt a nation?

And Micah 6:8 and Matthew 6:9–13 feed into my responses:

1. Righteousness is first God's, then ours (insofar as we are grounded in God's), and then society's (insofar as the fruit of our righteousness, grounded in God's, becomes manifest).
2. According to Micah 6:8, righteousness is doing justice, loving mercy, and walking humbly with God.
3. Righteousness exalts a nation by bringing to "earth as it is in heaven" the kingdom of God—a kingdom characterized by daily bread, forgiveness, and deliverance from evil (Matthew 6:9–13).

The chart reflects these basic answers, which will be developed further in the course of the chapters.

Figure 1. **The Promotion of Social Righteousness: An Overview**

Chapter 2 "*Thy kingdom come!*"	**Claiming the Kingdom:** The *Basis* of Social Righteousness	God's Promise ↓	God's Grace ↓	God's Love ↓
Chapter 3 "*Thy will be done*"	**Imagining the Kingdom:** The *Shape* of Social Righteousness	Do Justice ↓	Love Mercy ↓	Walk Humbly with God ↓
Chapter 4 "*On earth as it is in heaven*"	**Embodying the Kingdom:** The *Fruit* of Social Righteousness	Bread (all eat)	Forgiveness (all are reconciled)	Deliverance (all are free)

Now that we have located ourselves, packed our bags, and picked up our maps, we are ready to move forward on the journey itself. We begin by stepping out and finding sure footing on God's promise that the kingdom will come.

Study Questions

1. What do you think of when you hear the phrase "promotion of social righteousness"? What did the phrase mean a century ago, and how does it resonate and not resonate today?

2. Reflect on why and how the Presbyterian Church (U.S.A.) has maintained a commitment to promoting social righteousness.

3. What is social righteousness as it appears it will be promoted in the remainder of this book?

4. What does the Lord's Prayer have to say about the promotion of social righteousness?

Notes

1. *Book of Order,* Part II of *The Constitution of the Presbyterian Church (U.S.A.)* (Louisville: Office of the General Assembly, Presbyterian Church [U.S.A.], 2007), G-1.0200.
2. The aggressive and effective politics of the far right are not directed at changing the world as much as they are directed at preserving a space in which professing Christian believers can thrive in the midst of an otherwise (and inevitably) unrighteous world. In the terms of the Christian tradition, they emphasize what is known as the "civil use" of the law.
3. See, for example, soyouwanna.com/site/toptens/books/booksfull.html.
4. An important example of this is a recently reprinted book first published by Walter Rauschenbusch in 1907. Originally titled *Christianity and the Social Crisis,* the one-hundredth anniversary edition incorporates critical essays written by contemporary theologians under the title *Christianity and the Social Crisis in the 21st Century: The Classic That Woke Up the Church* (New York: HarperCollins, 2007).
5. My assistant, Laura Elly Hudson, did most of the research incorporated into this section of the chapter.
6. Jack B. Rogers and Robert E. Blade, "The Great Ends of the Church: Two Perspectives," *Journal of Presbyterian History* 76 no. 3 (Fall 1998): pp. 181–186.
7. *Book of Order,* G-1.0200, footnote 2.
8. The UPCNA, founded in 1858, united with the Presbyterian Church in the United States of America in 1958 to become the United Presbyterian Church in the United States of America (UPCUSA). The UPCUSA subsequently united with the Presbyterian Church in the United States (PCUS) in 1983.
9. Rogers and Blade, p. 182.
10. Ibid., p. 183.
11. Ibid., p. 184.
12. Ibid., p. 185.
13. The following points are drawn from an unpublished report on the minutes prepared by Hudson in 2008.
14. *Minutes of the Fifty-Second General Assembly of the United Presbyterian Church of North America,* Vol. 12 (Pittsburgh: United Presbyterian Board of Publication, 1910), p. 627.
15. Ibid.
16. Ibid., p. 659.
17. Ibid., p. 660.
18. Wallace N. Jamison, *United Presbyterian Story: A Centennial Study, 1858–1958* (Pittsburgh: Geneva Press, 1958), p. 97.
19. To read this article, go to witherspoonsociety.org/2004/social_creed.htm.
20. For more information on the new social creed, see "A Social Creed for the 21st Century" at pcusa.org/acswp/socialcreed21st.htm.
21. TeSelle, emphasis added.
22. A shorter version of the Lord's Prayer is found in Luke 11:2–4.
23. Praying the Lord's Prayer when we gather around the Table of the Kingdom of God is one way we remember, and benefit from, its eschatological character.
24. One theologian who makes this connection is Simone Weil. See "Concerning the Our Father," *Simone Weil Reader,* ed. George A. Panichas (Mt. Kisco, NY: Moyer Bell Limited, 1977), pp. 492–500.
25. Note the similarity, in this respect, to the Greatest Commandment.

2

Claiming the Kingdom: The *Basis* of Social Righteousness

Every time we pray the Lord's Prayer we express our desire that social righteousness be promoted. "Thy kingdom come!" we demand. When we say these words, if we remember that we are demanding something of God, our knees might begin to tremble. Who are we to be issuing imperatives to God? The answer to this question is both simple and impossible to fathom: We are God's children. We are encouraged[1] to demand certain things of God because—and only because—God is "our Father" who has made specific, extravagant promises to us.

The promise, grace, and love of God provide the basis for the church's promotion of social righteousness. While good arguments for working for a just society are often founded in active recognition of basic human rights and dignity, the church claims a more fundamental license for its work. It is what God wills. "Let justice roll down like waters, and righteousness like an ever-flowing stream" (Amos 5:24). It is what God commands. "Love your neighbor as yourself" (Mark 12:31). And most importantly, it is consistent with whom God created and redeemed us to be. "For we are what he has made us, created in Christ Jesus for good works, which God prepared beforehand to be our way of life" (Ephesians 2:10).

In short, the reason the church promotes social righteousness is not because everyone deserves to be treated justly, or because Jesus did so (and we should follow his example), or because it is in our best interest, given that what goes around comes around. The church's call to promote social righteousness cannot be fully accounted for by appeal to humanitarian arguments, pious intentions, or practical considerations. If it could, it would simply be another—and probably quite worthy—humanitarian endeavor, committed to devoting the best possible effort to accomplishing whatever can reasonably be done if we put our minds to it, make a few sacrifices, and volunteer our share of time and energy.

In contrast to this, the church's promotion of social righteousness is not grounded in us, but in God. It is not undertaken because every human being somehow deserves to be treated justly, but because a grace-full God has revealed to us that even those who are undeserving are fully included. It is not engaged because we are somehow obligated to share a little of the great bounty that God has given us, but because the triune God who is love (see 1 John 4:8b) has blessed all of God's children with everything God has. " 'You are always with me, and all that is mine is yours' " (Luke 15:31b).

We cannot remind each other too often, as partners in the work of promoting social righteousness, that the basis of our work is God and not ourselves. To forget is to be tempted away from the kingdom, toward building towers of our own design (see Genesis 11), toward striving to be little versions of the Messiah. To forget is to risk burning out. To forget is, in short, to sin. If we are to participate in the kingdom of God, rather than creating our own kingdoms, we need to remember that the promise, grace, and love of God provide the basis for social righteousness.

God's Promise

Our first child, Alexander, was born a little over five years ago. As everyone told me ahead of time, and as I believed, I had no idea. I had no idea that I could want to give more than the entirety of myself to a person who didn't even know his or my name. I had no idea that I could, in the grip of such a connection, be so free. Minutes after Xander was born, my husband, Bill, stood at the end of the bed and took him in his arms. "I am your daddy," he said, looking down, eyes full of tears, at that little face. "I am your daddy, and I am going to take care of you." Promises made. Promises made freely and absurdly. Promises about giving everything—everything we have. Two days later, when we were back at home, I found myself standing over Xander's crib. "This is your house," I whispered to him. "12406 Adelphi Cove. Your house. Your family." Somehow, I had the overwhelming sense that it could never be too early to start letting him know.

In baptizing infants, we tell them their address long before they are able to understand. "You belong here," we tell them, "and this place and these people belong to you. We belong to each other because we all belong to God. We are, together, the brothers and sisters of Christ. We are God's beloved children, and you are God's beloved child."

This is a tough concept to grasp, not only for two-day-old Alexander and the infant being baptized but also for all of us. And to grasp it is one thing; to live in light of it is quite another. That is why the greatest leaders of the faith always exhort us to be intentional about engaging in reflection and in spiritual practices that remind us of who we are. "Remember your baptism!" urges Martin Luther. "Remember your baptism, and be thankful." Jesus himself tries to help us conceptualize, in a variety of ways, how our lives are inextricably intertwined with his. "I am the vine, you are the branches," he explains (John 15:5). "I am the gate through which there is pasture; the good shepherd who lays down his life for his sheep," he declares.[2] "This is my body, which is given for you," he insists, breaking a loaf of bread and offering it to his disciples. "Do this in remembrance of me" (Luke 22:19).

The work of promoting social righteousness is rightly engaged in the context of such remembering. When we truly know we are the children of God, we engage in works of love freely, as extensions of who we are rather than as obligations we are required to fulfill. "For my yoke is easy, and my burden is light," Jesus reminds us (Matthew 11:30). We who abide in Christ bring forth much fruit (see John 15:5). We who partake of Christ's body and blood are strengthened to go out into the world with love for God and neighbor.

Our good works, when they are the overflow of our participation in the life of God, through Christ, by the power of the Holy Spirit, are absolutely essential to the fulfillment of God's promise to bring the kingdom "on earth as it is in heaven." Surely it is clear that God's promises to be with us, in Christ, even "to the end of the age" (Matthew 28:20) cannot accomplish the church's work of promoting social righteousness simply by virtue of their existence. Unless God's promises are recognized and lived out, something crucial is not yet complete. While God's promises are our inheritance whether we acknowledge them or not, knowing the reassurance and challenge of them makes all the difference. I might have an inheritance of millions lying around in a bank account somewhere, but until I am aware of this and make intentional decisions about this money, its reality is— from the vantage point of my existence—almost a moot point.

Speaking of how important it is for us to know the objective reality that God is with us and for us in the person of Jesus Christ, Karl Barth points out that "reality which does not become truth for us obviously cannot affect us, however supreme may be its ontological dignity." Insisting that our recognition of God's claim on us is essential to the event of revelation, Barth further explains that "in Jesus Christ a Christian has already come into being, but in himself and his time he is always in the process of becoming."[3] To live with the reassurance and the challenge that comes with knowing the truth of God's promises is to live as those who are becoming new creatures; to act in the world as those who have been made new is to be vehicles through which all things become new. In short, our calling to promote social righteousness is grounded in this understanding, in our becoming who we are, in and through Jesus Christ, by the power of the Spirit.

Being and Becoming

How do we become who we already are in Jesus Christ? Although there are no "magic formulas" for accomplishing this, God has promised that God is not finished with us yet: We who have been justified are also in the process of being sanctified; the Holy Spirit is working in us to conform us to the image of the Son (see Romans 8:29). While we can do no more to sanctify ourselves than we can to justify ourselves, we can position ourselves to live more fully in recognition of all God has promised. One of my seminary professors identified this as "being enough of a person that God can find." This doesn't mean that God offers us a whole lot and that we have only to put in a little something to seal the deal. What it means is that our participation, our exercise of faith, is part and parcel of God's grace-full work on our behalf. In this understanding, faith and its associated spiritual practices are not responses to God's grace, but themselves the work of grace. Along these lines, Barth helpfully describes faith as "surplus grace." It is not something added to grace as the "little something" we need to provide. It is itself an integral part of God's grace-full work.

Just as faith is the way God's grace-full work of justification looks on us when we live in recognition of God's promises, so faithful participation in spiritual practices is the way God's sanctifying work looks from the vantage point of creaturely existence. Both faith and the engagement of spiritual practices are instances of "surplus grace"— manifestations of God's claim on us and of God's working in us. Both we and God are involved in the working out of our salvation, in our becoming who we are in Christ. As Paul says in Philippians 2, following his powerful testimony to the incarnation and exaltation of Jesus Christ, "Therefore, my beloved . . . work out your own salvation with fear and trembling; for it is God who is at work in you, enabling you both to will and to work for God's good pleasure" (vv. 12–13).

Prayer: Holding God to Account

A primary way we "work out our salvation" is through prayer. It is tragic when we who are God's children tire of prayer and stop praying altogether, although this is a common experience for many of us. Thinking of my professor's instruction that we be "enough of person that God can find," I sometimes think of prayer as a time when I give the Holy Spirit a fighting chance to facilitate my becoming![4] In prayer, we remember we are God's children. In prayer, we claim God's promises. John Calvin called prayer "the chief exercise of faith . . . by which we daily receive God's benefits."[5] In prayer, we hold God to account in such a way that we become more of who we really are even as we insist God be true to who we know God is. For Calvin (and Paul, for that matter[6]) the relationship between faith and prayer is a chicken-and-egg kind of thing. We pray as people of faith, and in prayer we are assured in our faith. Faith spawns prayer; prayer deepens faith; all is a work of grace that "seals in our hearts," through the work of the Holy Spirit, the promise, in Christ, of God's benevolence.[7] Calvin thought it was absolutely extraordinary—a primary manifestation of our identity, as God's children—that we could pray to God about anything at any time and find reassurance.

"Our Father"

Too often we forget how downright astounding it is that we are invited by Jesus to pray in the posture of children laying claim to the promises of a parent. While it is unclear, according to New Testament scholars, how ordinary people of faith in Jesus' time would have addressed God, it is clear that we have generally lost sight of how outlandish it is to address the omnipotent, omnipresent, eternal Creator of the universe in the most intimate and relational of terms. "Our Father," Jesus teaches us to pray. Of all the ways Jesus could have begun the prayer, he leads with this. Not with an affirmation of God's majesty and power, but with claiming God's familial relationship with us.

To address the omnipotent Creator of the universe as "Father" is nothing short of scandalous. It immediately challenges any misconception we might have had that the transcendent God would remain only at a distance from us, or that to be godlike is benevolently to reward, punish, or forgive on the basis of faithful service or heartfelt contrition. It also immediately challenges any misconception we might have had that we can stay at a distance from God, doing what we are supposed to do, asking for forgiveness when we mess up, and saying "thank you" as much as possible, just to stay on the safe side. To say

"Our Father" is to evoke God's promise to be with us. It is both to be comforted in our loneliness and challenged in our complacency.

The first word of the Lord's Prayer—the possessive pronoun "our"—immediately joins us in relationship to Jesus Christ, that One who was never bashful about claiming promises made to him by God. Consider, for example, Jesus' prayer found in John 17, in which he asks that he be glorified and that the disciples be sanctified, joy-filled, and united. Jesus also holds God to account when God doesn't seem to be keeping God's promises. "My God, my God, why have you forsaken me?" Jesus candidly asks, in anguish because he has relied on God's promise to be with him and does not understand why this promise has been broken (Matthew 27:46). Jesus consistently expects God to bless (see Matthew 5:1–12; Luke 6:20–23), to heal (see John 9:1–12), to forgive (see Luke 23:34), and to deliver (see Matthew 6:13).

"Our Father," spoken by our Savior and brother Jesus Christ, reminds us of our abiding in him and his in us; of our identification, through the waters of baptism, in his life, death, and resurrection; of our status as adopted children, as fellow heirs. The first word of the Lord's Prayer counters faulty reasoning that argues Jesus (but not us) could get away with audaciously demanding the promises of God because he (and not us) is the Son of God. To pray "Our Father" is to claim the promises Jesus claimed as the only Son of God who has made us sons and daughters with him.

Expecting God to Be God

The fundamental reason we confidently claim the promises God makes to us is because God always follows through on who God is. Theologians like to put it this way: God's acts are always consistent with God's being. As Barth habitually reminds us, "God is God." What this means is that the God who is "Father" will always act the way a father or mother will act in their best moments of fatherliness or motherliness. Unlike human parents, whose acts are not always consistent with who they are as parents, God "Our Father" will always follow through. Unlike human fathers and mothers, God "Our Father" will always keep God's promises. It is precisely because we believe God's acts are always in sync with God's being that we rely on, and lay claim to, the promises God makes.

This same belief also leads us to be deeply troubled when God seems to act in ways inconsistent with who God is. As the children of God who know who God is, we faithfully cry out to God in the face of brokenness and unfulfilled promises. With the suffering psalmist, we tell God: "Rouse yourself!" (Psalm 44:23). This primal demand takes seriously God's promise to love, to heal, and to protect. It is a cry of faith that claims God for who God is in a moment in which God does not appear to be acting true to form.

The idea that God is all-powerful is too often falsely evoked as justification for everything that happens, as though the point of God's sovereignty is that God can do anything God wants, and we just have to accept it as OK. This way of thinking is inconsistent with the character of God as revealed to us in the triune God's particular acts (e.g., creating us, redeeming us, and strengthening us in love). From the vantage point of our creaturely existence, then, quite a different stance should accompany our confession of the divine sovereignty. That is, rather than goading us to accept that all that happens is OK, our confession that God is sovereign leads us prophetically to renounce anything inconsistent with promises made by this God who is always God. When a child dies, or a terrorist strikes, or a cancer is found, our conviction that God is sovereign, and that therefore the promises of this God have to be a sure thing, leads us emphatically to name what is *not* OK.

"Rouse yourself!" we pray. Again, we pray it precisely because God is sovereign, and because this God promises something specific about every tear being wiped away from every eye, and because when a God who is sovereign makes such a promise we had better be able to count on it—even when we're having trouble seeing how it is playing out. And so the faith-full response to be made, by the children of the sovereign God who have claimed the promises made by this God, is to insist that God wake up, come through, and be exactly who God is.

"Not Somehow, But Triumphantly"

I had a friend in seminary who would put a sign that read "not somehow, but triumphantly" on the door of her dormitory room during every final examinations period. While the rest of us thought the best we could do was embrace a "survival" mentality until our papers were turned in, Michelle insisted on claiming God's promises in the midst of it all. She did not mean by this something silly, such as God would enable us all to get "triumphant" A's regardless of how much attention we gave to our coursework. She meant that we children of God should live as though God's promises are the operative reality even when life is difficult. Each morning of reading week and finals, stumbling out of my room in a studious, sleep-deprived state to make my way down the hall to our shared bathroom, I was confronted by Michelle's proclamation of the good news. I was reminded that these promises are not only about some other world, but also about this world—this world right now, today. That sign nudged me toward being the person I really am: a child of God, not a hypocrite or a would-be imposter. I was moved by the Spirit of the Living God, who melted me and molded me back into that child who trusts her loving father and mother and, therefore, expects—even demands—triumph.

As Jesus teaches, and as many of the men and women of faith in Scripture exemplify: "Unless you have the faith of a child, you will not enter the kingdom of heaven." It's funny that we tend to think of a child's faith as simple—as a faith that never questions because it only trusts. My experience, as the mother of three- and five-year-old children, is that the trust my children have in me does nothing to temper their asking of questions or their making demands but in fact almost gives them carte blanche. I tell them I will take them to the park later and they remind me of this promise precisely because they believe I will keep it. And their conviction that I will take them, even though I haven't taken them yet, leads them to ask (over and over and over again! Like the friend in the parable in Luke 11:5–10, knocking on the door for bread . . .), "When are we going? When?"

While God's promises clearly benefit God's children, the reason we lay claim to them is, first and foremost, because they are true. We believe God is forgiving. When we sin and lay claim to God's promise to forgive, our sin does not incapacitate us. We live in forgiving relationship to others and are set free by the decision to live as those who have been set free. We believe God is a God of healing. So when we witness or experience suffering and lay claim to God's promise to heal, our pain does not diminish us. We renounce that which should not be, demanding and discerning the presence of God, refusing to replace our conviction that God is sovereign with logical explanations for why there is pain.

If we based the way we live solely on what is beneficial, we would inevitably create gods of our own making rather than living in relationship to the God who is God. But we lucked out, so to speak. What we profess to be true is also beneficial to us in our journeys through this life.

One of the figures in Scripture who manifests such childlike faith is Job. His trust never wavers, nor does his insistence that God be true to who God is and what God has promised. "I know that my Redeemer lives," he asserts in the midst of his suffering, calling on God to come through (see Job 19:25). For forty-two chapters he holds tenaciously to his conviction that, because God is both sovereign and good, he will not be forgotten. It is precisely because Job believes so firmly that his forgotten-ness is an aberration that will be corrected that he is able to name his forgotten-ness. He is able to complain to God about what has happened. He is free to register his confusion about his circumstances, about the fact that God doesn't appear yet to have kept God's promises. While his friends go to great lengths trying to adjust their understandings of what God has promised in order to make sense of it all, Job maintains his childlike faith. "You promised," he insists, "and we haven't gone to the park, yet. But I know you will still take me, and so I will keep reminding you, as your irrepressibly confident (because I know I am loved) child."

With the Sure Faith of Confident Children

John Calvin encourages all Christian believers to pray in the childlike way Job prayed, and I am convinced this has to do with Calvin's uncompromising embrace of the divine sovereignty. It is because the God who has claimed us is sovereign and because the sovereign God has claimed us, Calvin believes, that we are free to pray to God at any time about anything. Calvin urges Christian believers always to pray from a sincere sense of want and with confident hope.[8]

Certainly, Calvin's insistence that we need to pray with the sure faith of confident children is influenced not only by his conviction that God is sovereign, but by his reflection on the way Jesus taught us to pray—that is, the Lord's Prayer itself. He reminds us that the very idea of finite, sinful creatures addressing the all-holy Creator of the universe as "Our Father" is simply outrageous. "With what confidence would anyone address God as 'Father'?" he asks. "Who would break forth into such rashness as to claim for himself [or herself] the honor of a [child] of God unless we had been adopted as children of grace in Christ?"[9] "Clearly, in and through Christ we have been adopted," he reminds us, and therefore will never be forgotten[10] and can even expect to receive "good gifts."[11] Because we are—alongside our brother, Jesus Christ— the children of God, even our sin may not be used as an excuse for being reticent in prayer. "Let us not pretend that we are justly rendered timid by the consciousness of sins," Calvin exhorts us, since God our Father stands ready to embrace us out of "an abundance of fatherly compassion" even before we have "asked for pardon."[12] Not even our sin may stand in the way of claiming God's promises to feed us, to forgive us, to deliver us from that which pulls us away from the reality of the coming kingdom.

And neither may the sins of others subvert God's promises. This is why, even when someone is stealing our bread, we claim God's promise that bread will be provided. This is why, in contexts in which forgiveness seems at least impractical (if not impossible), we continue to insist on forgiveness as a way of life. This is why we ask for deliverance from any distortion of what God desires, believing that God's kingdom will come "on earth as it is in heaven."

God's promises are not conditional. God loves us, no matter what. Grace has no requirements. We say those words all the time, but they are difficult to live into. How do we live into those truths we talk about so readily? How do we begin to lay claim to God's promises in such a way that they—and not our relative worth or unworthiness—dictate the course we follow as those called to be salt and light in the world?

Those are difficult questions to answer. We have already addressed, in this chapter, why we are free to claim God's promises. In short, we may claim God's promises because, and only because, we are the children of the God who has claimed us. But knowing this isn't always enough. Often it is difficult to live into our identity as the beloved children of God. The following three subsections discuss why this is the case: First, it is because we don't feel entitled to the promises God makes us (and are, therefore, deeply troubled when anyone uses the language of "rights"). And second, it is because we feel entitled to what we think are God's promises, which are actually false promises of our own making.

Our Reticence: Missing Out on the Promises

When we are reticent to stake our claim as the brothers and sisters of Jesus Christ, we risk missing out on the abundant life that is our inheritance as children of God. At first glance, it might make sense to us to renounce all sense of entitlement. After all, we are not Jesus. But to engage our spiritual journeys as those who at the same time confess that we "belong to God . . . in life and in death"[13] and think putting aside all claims to promises is a sign of spiritual maturity is, in actuality, deeply problematic. If we do not live as those to whom God has made promises, our claims to belong to God have little significance. Analogously, to be married without expectation that promises made should be kept is not to live in covenantal relationship. To have a close friend from whom we never demand anything is not to have a close friend. To belong to someone is to expect what has been promised; to live in gratitude for what has been, what is, and what is to come; and to grieve when promises are broken.

One reason we may at first glance associate demanding the promises of God with spiritually immature behavior is because we have mistakenly confused *promises* with popular conceptions of *rights*.

Philosophical discussions on the subject of human rights are exceedingly rich, with debates on important questions such as: What rights are "natural" and what rights are acquired on the basis of merit? And, what rights should never be taken away, even if honoring them in relation to certain individuals is likely to put others in jeopardy? Some reflection by people of faith on when the language of rights should be appreciated might help remove barriers to our claiming of God's promises.

Yet sometimes there are good reasons to be suspicious of discourse focused solely on the claiming of rights. Reference to those seeking their rights often carries a negative connotation. This is commonly due to latent or blatant prejudices against persons from minority groups who are rightfully voicing concerns about their place in society. Perhaps it is also because we live in a highly litigious society in which we are consistently subjected to, for example, television commercials featuring lawyers who, eager for our business, scream at us about knowing our rights in relationship to any number of important or incidental matters.

The notion of someone insisting on his or her rights is sometimes associated with a lack of a self-sacrificing spirit, and even with an annoying degree of selfishness. The posture of a rights-seeker, stereotypically portrayed, is antithetical to that of a model Christian believer. We, as disciples of Jesus Christ, are called to put aside our own agendas in obedience to the will of God, to submit to one another out of reverence for Christ (see Ephesians 5:21), to deny ourselves, pick up our own crosses, and follow him (see Matthew 16:24). With such mandates in play, rehearsal of rights seems at least inappropriate and perhaps even absurd. To think of God as our Father, implying that we have certain rights as the children of that father, is woefully off track in this mode of thinking. And the category of "promise" might seem mildly disrespectful and presumptuous, too close to enter comfortably. After all, the omnipotent God could not possibly owe us anything, whether on the basis of rights or promises, we might logically enough think. To think of God as our Father, as in any sense obligated to us, seems absurd. Certainly, God does not owe us anything. We are saved by grace alone, not of ourselves (see Ephesians 2:8). We should be grateful for what we have that we do not deserve, rather than demanding even more of God.

There are things that are basically correct, and things that are dead wrong, about this line of argument. What is basically correct is that it doesn't hurt, every now and then, to remember our unworthiness. In our so-called entitlement culture, a healthy dose of remembering what we don't deserve might be beneficial to most of us on many days. And the logic of it all is mechanically impeccable: We don't deserve what God has promised and, therefore, have no right to demand anything. What is wrong about this argument is that it argues from our unworthiness for a necessary withdrawal from God's promises. Theologically speaking, such an ordering is a disaster. God's promises are not made on the basis of our worthiness, nor are they kept only consequent to our good behavior. Whatever social righteousness is about, it cannot be something we are beholden to achieve before we are entitled to that which is promised. The ordering is precisely the reverse: It is because God has promised us something that we are free, therefore, to be righteous. It is because the promises are true regardless of our behavior that our unworthiness is brought home to us. How can we—the way we behave—be so loved? How can we—we who are sinners—be grace-full participants in the life and work of God? To consider worth before promise is never to know the promise; to claim promise first is to know at once that one is both beloved and unworthy.

Revisiting Rights

For those of us who worry that claiming God's promises looks a little too similar to claiming our rights, it might be useful to challenge the stereotypical view that anyone using language of rights is inevitably selfish. As Christian believers, we are called to be sensitive to the reasons people are demanding or angry as an extension of our love for them, our neighbors. And if we are paying any attention at all to what is going on in the world, we will recognize the persistence of inequalities that are devastating to the flourishing of human life. The unequal distribution of resources is so defining that it seems, for those who attend to the dynamics, that everything will have to change for anything significant to change. To illustrate this: The old adage about teaching a poor person to fish, rather than giving him or her a fish to eat, really isn't that simple. It is probably true that if a poor person is given a fish he or she won't be hungry for a day, as the wisdom runs. But knowing how to fish doesn't guarantee that a person will never be hungry again. Of course, one could argue, the saying is mainly a metaphor—its point is that we need to do more than simply give handouts to the hungry. But think of how difficult it would be to set up a system in which everyone who was once hungry is now not hungry because they are equipped to obtain food. Significant questions would need to be answered:

- Who is going to do the teaching?
- Who is going to pay for the fishing poles and the bait?
- Who is going to make sure we get the pollution out of the water and pass legislation that protects fish populations from being wiped out, so that there are fish to be fished by those who have learned to fish?

And some philosophical, ethical, and theological issues hit even closer to home, such as:

- It is hard enough to motivate those of us who are richer than others to hand over even a few fish. And now we're supposed to work up the energy to teach the poor to fish?
- What happens when we find out the poor already know how to fish, or that we who can eat all the fish we want are actually being fed by those who are hungry?
- Do we apologize and give the fish back?
- Or do we pay more for the fish, and therefore have fewer of them, so the fisher folk have more money to buy food?

If this list of questions seems exhausting or frustrating to those of us who get exasperated with language of rights, perhaps we can better imagine the exhaustion and frustration (as well as the sense of urgency) had by many who insist their rights are not being honored.

Entitlement: The False "Promise" of Cheap Grace

Perhaps it seems strange to place so much emphasis on our resistance to claiming God's promises in a context often identified as a culture of entitlement. Isn't the issue more that we claim too much of God? That we perceive ourselves as overly worthy, rather than irredeemably unworthy?

I hypothesize that those who would take time to read this book are those who struggle less with the sin of assuming they are entitled and more with the sin of not claiming the promises that are ours as the children of God. It seems that those who operate with a strong sense of entitlement would not be as interested in actively promoting social righteousness for the benefit of all.

Still, even those of us who struggle with our own sense of unworthiness have our self-important moments. Fearing the depth of our own insecurities, we construct false selves that manipulate and demand. Hurt by systems that further disempower us, we leverage whatever rights we technically have to get less than what we really need.

What we really need, from God and from one another, is not a little more (and then a little more than that, until we have it "all"). What we need is that which matters most: to belong, to be forgiven, to be loved. No level of self-importance or entitlement can effectively secure such things. Even those with the most heightened sense of entitlement eventually discover that belonging, forgiveness, and love cannot be forcefully obtained, for they are pure gift. And so they either repent or are forced to settle for what they assume is deliverable by God and by others.

In a classic (though probably overused) example, a Christian believer feels such a strong sense of entitlement that he or she treats God as though God is a kind of cosmic gumball machine. Put in the prayer "coin," and the blessing comes out. If he prays for a parking space, he brags, he gets one. If she asks for help on an exam, she insists, God gives it. These people explain, "Why not? After all, God wants God's children to be blessed—we only have to ask."

Such an entitlement posture is problematic, in part, because it attempts to form God's promises around the items on our to-do lists rather than honoring God's promises as the bases upon which our lives are ordered. To claim, as Calvin did, that we can pray about anything at any time is quite a different thing than to claim that God will get us a parking space whenever we want it. We might pray for a parking space as children who are confident that God cares about even our more petty concerns. Ideally, our prayer then recalls us to living as God's children regardless of whether we find a good place to park our car.

To demand things of God out of a strong sense of entitlement is to misunderstand the inexhaustible character of the promises, grace, and love of God. Dietrich Bonhoeffer, along these lines, criticizes those who treat God's grace as though it is cheap. To understand, as a corollary to God's unconditional love, that we may therefore do nothing for God or for others, is to misunderstand the character of the divine love. To assume that to be children of God means we get everything we want is to forget our call to discipleship.[14]

The next major section of this chapter develops this idea further by presenting grace not as cheap, and not even as costly, but as completely other than all our economic, transactional ways of understanding. When grace is truly known, unworthiness and worthiness become nonissues and we are free to serve one another in love, rather than out of obligation.

Claiming Hope

Human creatures that sin and suffer have a need to claim what God has promised or they are liable to be left without hope. Without the promise of forgiveness, a sinner can move on with life only by minimizing his or her sinfulness or by doing whatever penance seems to counteract it. Without the promise that every tear will be wiped away from every eye, a sufferer can continue living either by shrugging her shoulders at the way life is or by believing he must have done something to bring the suffering upon himself and, therefore, can improve matters with better behavior. Minimizing sin, doing penance, shrugging shoulders, and acting out of guilt may be useful means for surviving this life, given the realities of sin and suffering. But living hope-fully entails more than merely surviving. It means, in fact, thriving—living the abundant life that Jesus Christ desires us to have.

How is it that we are so certain that God's promises will come to be? We are certain not because God has the all-time highest known credit score or an indisputable reputation for "coming through," even when times are tough. Let's be honest: There are too many times when bread is not immediately in evidence. On the basis of evidence alone, one might argue that God sometimes keeps God's promises, but not that God always does. There are points in our lives, and in this world, when the keeping of God's promises cannot be seen, and so we are left with the promise of the cross. At these difficult junctures, we cling to the promise that God is with us now, even before resurrection—right now, in these moments of suffering, before the tears are wiped away. Claiming the promise of God's presence, we pray for the fulfillment of another promise, demanding that the kingdom come to earth as it is in heaven. When we pray in this way, we reflect confidence not only that the promises of God will one day somehow be kept, but that God will ever continue to be who we know God to be: the God of grace; the God who loves.

God's Grace

I memorized a standard definition of *grace* in sixth-grade confirmation class at the First Presbyterian Church of Babylon, New York. "Grace is unmerited favor," I was taught.

But what is "unmerited favor"?

Well, let's see: "Favor" is associated with "approval" or "kindness." And something "unmerited" is not earned or deserved.

So, grace as unmerited favor is approval or kindness that is not earned or deserved.

I suppose that explains why my students thank me "for the grace" when I give them twenty-four-hour extensions on their papers for all sorts of pressing and less pressing reasons. It's their way of saying they recognize that they got something they didn't earn, that I have been kind to them when—given the supposed tit-for-tat rules that govern the cosmos—I apparently didn't have to be.

We are in very big theological trouble if we understand my offering of an extension as anything like the grace of God. Going even further, I offer the following judgment: We *are* in very big theological trouble *because* we *do* understand the grace of God in terms of something like supersized kindness. In brief, we have compromised our understanding of grace (1) because it is impossible to comprehend and (2) because—when we do catch a glimpse of it—it is impossible to bear. When we reduce our understanding of grace to something manageable, we set aside the very heart of the gospel: that is, that the impossibility of relationship with God has been made possible, in and through Jesus Christ, by the power of the Holy Spirit.

To set aside *grace* as the basis for our work of promoting social righteousness is to take matters into our own hands—as though we are somehow capable of emulating God's kindness, but on a smaller scale! When we forget that the promises of God are *impossible* by any standards we know, we risk living not in creative freedom, but with the albatross of having to construct a "new and improved" world on our backs. These thoughts need further unpacking.

Supersized Kindness

Our lives are filled with evidence that grace is compromised because it is a concept that is incomprehensible to us. The idea that we might receive something that we don't deserve is alien to us at best. It is arguably unfair—why should anyone get something that he or she doesn't deserve? As I write these words in the context of the U.S. recession, tension over failed mortgages, and whether taxpayer dollars should be utilized to save them, is palpable. Even the most benevolent Americans want to be convinced that their money is helping those who *deserve* help. If we could simply give everyone what they deserve—if we could allocate resources "fairly" in this regard—the world would be a much better place. If only we could be as deserving, fair, and correct as the elder son in Luke 15, everything would be just fine. We don't need the unreasonableness and lack of boundaries manifested by the father toward the younger son. In fact, we'd do better without such dysfunctional behavior, if what we are after is creating a just, fair, socially righteous world.

Further evidence is found in the fact that certain translations of the Bible avoid use of the term *grace*. In the spirit of offering a more readable translation, the Contemporary English Version of Scripture, for example, omits the term *grace* altogether, replacing it with more understandable terms and phrases such as *kindness* and *better than we deserve*. Two comparisons of translations from the NRSV and the CEV illustrate this point. The first, Romans 5:15, shows the CEV's use of *kindness* instead of *grace:*

But the free gift is not like the trespass. For if the many died through the one man's trespass, much more surely have the *grace* of God and the free gift in the *grace* of the one man, Jesus Christ, abounded for the many. —Romans 5:15 (NRSV)	But the gift that God was kind enough to give was very different from Adam's sin. That one sin brought death to many others. Yet in an even greater way, Jesus Christ alone brought God's gift of *kindness* to many people. —Romans 5:15 (CEV)

While *kindness* is, undoubtedly, more understandable than *grace,* it misleads us in significant ways in understanding the character of God's claim on us and our relationship to God. These will be considered in more detail, especially insofar as responding to what we know of kindness can infuse us with a sense of obligation that drives us to work for social righteousness, rather than inviting us to engage the work as those who have been set free (see John 8:36).

The second text, Ephesians 2:8–9, shows how the CEV avoids use of the term *grace* by substituting the idea that we have been treated by God *much better than we deserve:*

For by *grace* you have been saved through faith, and this is not your own doing; it is the gift of God—not the result of works, so that no one may boast.
—Ephesians 2:8–9 (NRSV)

You were saved by faith in God, who treats us *much better than we deserve*. This is God's gift to you, and not anything you have done on your own. It isn't something you have earned, so there is nothing you can brag about.
—Ephesians 2:8–9 (CEV)

While again the CEV translation is probably more understandable to the average reader than the NRSV translation, the question is whether what is being communicated is consistent with who God is, and what the relationship of God to the world is like. To think of ourselves as being treated by God as "much better than we deserve" misses the point, since the God of grace loves us without any attention whatsoever to our deservingness or undeservingness. In other words, "better than we deserve" implies that we deserve *something* and that we actually receive *more* than whatever it is we've earned. This treats grace almost as though it is a "tip" of some sort, rather than a perfect gift given freely by a lover who would not pause for an instant to consider the beloved's deservingness or undeservingness.

In our drive to make things understandable, we unwittingly compromise on the core of what they are about. And the translators of the CEV are not the only ones guilty of this. Thinking back to my confirmation definition of *grace* as "unmerited favor," I realize that it is also portrayed in transactional terms. Whatever committee wrote the definition reflected thoughtfully on the fact that grace is *more* than *more than we deserve;* it is something that is, in fact, *not deserved at all*. But at some point, the definers and their heirs seem to have dropped the ball, giving in to the pressure to describe grace in manageable terms. I say this because in the definition grace is known only in relation to (the absence of) merit. But in reality grace is not related to merit at all, neither positively nor negatively. In other words, it is not that we *don't* deserve grace any more than we do deserve it. Whether we deserve it or not is utterly irrelevant to the existence of grace. Grace is not best described, then, as "unmerited favor." More simply put, it is "God's favor." Period.

Such a definition will probably not satisfy us. We will want to tag to the end of it something like: "even though we don't deserve it." It is almost as if we are incapable of imagining a reality that can escape the categories of "deserving" and "undeserving" altogether. It is almost as if we can find no way of thinking that is outside our constraining paradigms of exchange.

Related to this, it is clear we are thinking about grace as something we get rather than a concept that describes the character of God's posture toward us. We realize that what we're getting with grace is more than anything we can ask or imagine (see Ephesians 3:20), and to the degree that we realize this we simultaneously recognize our own unworthiness. "Amazing grace," we sing, "how sweet the sound, that saved a *wretch* like me!"[15] (emphasis added). And recognizing our unworthiness is beneficial until we draw from our experience of it in the attempt to constrain the workings of grace: not God's *unmerited* favor, but God's favor. And what God's favor is all about, as it turns out, is not primarily getting things (e.g., salvation, forgiveness, abundant life). It is about something even more fundamental: God being with and for us. To *favor* someone is to *be* for them, to stand with them, to believe in them, to make a particular claim on them, to call them by name (see Isaiah 43:1).

This poses a "conceptual problem."[16] How is it that the God who "has measured the waters in the hollow of his hand" (Isaiah 40:12) is at the same time the Good Shepherd who seeks out the one sheep gone missing from a hundred (see Luke 15:1–7)? How is it that the God before whom "the hills sing together for joy" (Psalm 98:8) is at the same time a woman who sweeps her whole house, determined to find the one coin that has gone missing (see Luke 15:8–10)? What does it mean that the Almighty God "emptied" God's self *not* to set the stage for a grandiose display about God's cosmic supremacy, but to ensure that *every* knee would bend; that *every* tongue would confess; that each and every one would *know* that they are claimed by the One who came, and died, and rose, for all (see Philippians 2)? How is it that the One who is Lord of all, without need of any particular one of us, refuses to leave any of us behind? "Lift up your eyes on high and see," the prophet Isaiah insists, inviting us to ponder this conceptual problem that lies at the heart of our faith. "Who created these? He who brings out their host and numbers them, calling them all by name; because he is great in strength, mighty in power, *not one is missing*" (Isaiah 40:26, emphasis added).

Pondering the absurdity of this conceptual problem, it is no wonder that we forego grace, instead constructing more comprehensible ways of understanding God's relationship to us. Very few of us have the faith of Abram, who responds in faith when God shows him the stars, promising him that he will not be forgotten (see Genesis 15). Very few of us have the faith of Mary, accepting that God makes the impossible possible, committing ourselves to the task of bearing God to the world even though we know ourselves to be virgins (see Luke 2). And so we smooth over the conceptual problem, in the name of making our beliefs accessible and, therefore, marketable. God's grace becomes God's "great kindness"; the "impossible" becomes that which is "hard to pull off, but perfectly achievable as long as we 'do our best and let God take care of the rest'"; "every knee" bowing and "every tongue" confessing and "not one is missing" become "a good number of knees" or "a respectable number of tongues" or "more than we might expect to be there." The sky-full of stars becomes, in our perception, practically dark. We live with a kind of persistent but reasonable hope that we might be able to make out a star or two, if we stare up into the darkness long enough, squint our eyes a little, and really work at it. We have given up, without even knowing we have done so, on claiming God's promise that everything God has is ours (see Luke 15). We have given up, in the name of being realistically optimistic, on claiming the kingdom of God.

Why is it that we so readily let go of that which is promised, especially since—presumably—it is that which we most desire? Why is it so difficult to have the faith of Abram, living in the light of that infinite excess of stars? One reason might be because, when we *have* managed to believe, we have been disappointed. We have found ourselves on Mt. Moriah, and no ram has shown up to preserve our hopes. And we don't want to be disappointed again.

Another reason might be because we are afraid of looking like fools. Setting our expectations absurdly high and then being disappointed looks foolish, in a world blatantly characterized by broken promises and subsequent disappointment. We should know better. Who wants to look foolish, on top of being disappointed?

In addition, we so-called "postmoderns" set our expectations low because we know very well what happens, on a grand historical scale, when we set them high. We remember Hiroshima and Auschwitz; we worry about global warming, cloning, and global recession. The technological advancements that improve life are as often used for life's destruction. The stocks that were rising are worth less now than when we first purchased them. If we set our expectations low, we figure, we will experience fewer disappointments. And we will appear more reasonable, more in control, and far less foolish than those who hope for too much.

Grace: Maddening Impossibility

The nineteenth-century Danish philosopher Søren Kierkegaard appreciates those who set their expectations high, but not too high. Those who expect what is possible—those who hope—are great. They are the ones who try hard, who don't give up easily, and who are good at problem solving. They are the ones who search the sky relentlessly, even when others have given up on it as star-less. They are the ones most likely to become our heroes, guiding us toward that which is highly unlikely, difficult to achieve, but still possible—if we are willing to put our minds and energies toward it.

But Kierkegaard proposes an additional category. While those who expect what is possible—those who hope—are great, those who expect the impossible—those whose hope takes the form of madness—these are the greatest of all.[17] What could Kierkegaard possibly mean by this, and how does this insight help us grasp the ungraspability of grace?

More than a hundred years after Kierkegaard wrote these words, Joe Darion wrote the lyrics to "The Impossible Dream." The song is first sung, in *Man of La Mancha,* by Don Quixote—an eccentric personality who insists he will strive for what is right and what is loving "no matter how hopeless" his dream for these things might be. As it turns out, Don Quixote is nuts. His niece, Antonia, is among those who spend the play trying to get him committed.

While our culture values Lance Armstrong types, it doesn't much value Don Quixotes. To dream the "highly unlikely but still somehow imaginable and attainable" dream is commendable, but to dream the "impossible dream" is laughable. To be a go-getter who insists on gazing at the night sky until she is able to make out a star or two is to be an optimist; to imagine a sky-full of stars on a night that is pitch dark is to be delusional.[18] To believe the world can be a better place, with less pain and greater honoring of life, is to be a spiritual leader. To envision every tear being wiped away from every eye and everyone enjoying the fruits of their own labors (see Isaiah 65) is to be a fanatic.

Maybe this is why being realistic has become almost a religious value in our culture. College students in the United States are increasingly encouraged not to pursue degrees in the humanities, but to study subjects that will more certainly get them jobs, and jobs that are higher paying. Educators find themselves players in a system that increasingly ridicules learning for its own sake, demanding lists of goals, projected outcomes, and means of assessment that take so much literal and emotional energy that creating the sacred classroom space in which unexpected and impossible "ahas" can occur is considered radical (and, of course, foolish) activity. Women are increasingly pressured *not* to try to "have it all," but rather to choose to spend a decade or so of their lives *either* raising children *or* climbing the corporate ladder. The possibility that we could achieve the impossible—that we could create a new system in which all people, including mothers, could have adequate time both to work and to be with family—seems so "far out" to us that we merely laugh at its suggestion or comment gravely and sincerely that we really wish it could be so, *but* . . .

Ironically, even the unrealistic overspending of the last decade that led to our current economic crisis was done in the name of being realistic. It is our commitment to being realistic that led many of us to overpack our storehouses at the expense of others rather than foolishly envisioning and working toward a day when every stomach will be filled. We told ourselves it is important that we invest and grow assets, given the expected length of our lifetimes and the expected failure of the Social Security system. We assumed it was prudential to store up for ourselves treasures that are concrete, spacious, and/or at the technological cutting edge, assuring one another that we *deserve* to have the best quality of life possible. (Think of how many television ads, for example, played up the "you deserve it!" angle.) We rarely questioned—nor do we yet commonly question—the association of the best quality of life with wealth, rather than with, for example, having greater opportunity to think, share, or enjoy the company of family and friends. I think this is because we consider thinking, sharing, and fellowship to be allusive goods, compared to having wealth. Strong relationships are neither measurable nor manageable; they are possibly not even possible, given that they cannot be verified empirically. They are, therefore, not *realistic*.

Grace or Gratitude

Given the reality of our realism, it must be acknowledged that grace is not a likely basis for the work of promoting social righteousness. From a pragmatic point of view, it would be better if we scrapped the concept of grace and went with something a little more workable. Instead of saying, for example, that service to others adds nothing whatsoever to the gracious reality of God's love for us, this line of thinking would argue that we would do better to emphasize that people should be grateful for all God has done for them and live their lives accordingly. Work that promotes social righteousness could then be advanced as a kind of thank-you note to God. Because God has done so much for us, we could say, the least we can do is express our gratitude by doing a little something for others. If worse came to worst, and we who are Christian leaders had difficulty precipitating the kind of actions needed, we could offer a veiled threat that appears entirely biblical. "Don't be like those goats!" we could warn people, encouraging them to turn to Matthew 25. "It is not enough simply to believe. We've got to get out there and feed, and clothe, and visit, and improve things!"

However, to substitute gratitude for grace as the basis for promoting social righteousness is to take matters into our own hands. It is *not* that there is a problem with showing gratitude to God, with thanking God for what God has done and treating others accordingly. The problem comes when we understand our efforts to be grounded in our gratitude rather than in the benevolence of God that invites this gratitude. It is not the case that God has loved me and now it is up to me, in gratitude, to save the world. Such thinking forgets that the coming of the kingdom of God is not our doing, in any way, apart from the doing of God. Such thinking compromises on the fullness of God's promise by settling for that which is difficult, but still somehow manageable and achievable. Such thinking loses sight of the fact that works of love, done in faith, are not merely responses to the gracious acts of God, but are part and parcel of it. Such thinking reveals that we have ceased living as people of faith; we have forsaken watching for the radical in-breaking of God in our midst. Instead, we have succumbed to the burdened, hopeless theology of "doing our best" and "letting God take care of the rest."

Grace insists that God will take care of all of it *and* that we will be fully included in what God is up to. In and of ourselves we can do nothing *and* in and through the One we await we can do all things— even the impossible things that characterize the kingdom.

God's Love

How do we participate so completely in the love of God for us that our love spills over into works that promote social righteousness?

Unfortunately, we cannot count on human love translating into right actions. This is because our actions, even when we do love, are often erratic. We who love do not always act lovingly. We are not patient; we are not kind. We are envious; we are boastful; we are arrogant; we are rude. We insist on our own way; we are irritable and resentful (see 1 Corinthians 13:4–5). While love itself never fails, we who love fail all the time. There is often little continuity between who we are, as those who love, and how we act, as limited creatures struggling with sin. And, to complicate matters further, actions that appear loving do not necessarily imply the presence of love. They can, of course, be grounded in other less loving motives.

If we really want to understand how love spills over into works that promote social righteousness, we need to begin with reflection on God rather than with reflection on ourselves. God's actions, in contrast to ours, are always in perfect continuity with who God is. In and through God's acts on our behalf, we witness what overflowing love looks like. A claim absolutely fundamental to the Christian faith is that what God does for us is a revelation of God's very self. In other words, when God acts, God is being exactly who God is.

One of the wonderful implications of this is that we can come to know who God really is in and through God's acts on our behalf. I often think of it this way: While the actions of human beings may or may not reveal something altogether true about them, God's actions always reveal who God is. When God acts, God isn't simply "doing things" for us. Rather, God is reminding us that God *is* with and for us. As a father who runs to meet the prodigal is acting freely out of who he is as that child's father (see Luke 15:20), as a mother will not forsake her nursing child (see Isaiah 49:14–15), so God is being exactly who God is in creating us, becoming incarnate in the person of Jesus Christ, and interceding through the ministry of the Spirit.[19]

We can trust, therefore, that the God who creates us, redeems us, forgives us, and calls us, *is* Creator, Redeemer, Forgiver, Elector. God is not "going out of God's way" to do something for us, any more than the father is going out of his way to welcome the prodigal home, or the nursing mother is going out of her way to feed her baby. To welcome, and to nurse, *is* the way of the father and the mother in relationship to their beloved children. God, in all of God's beautiful acts, is being precisely who God is, was, and always will be—in all of God's fullness.

This is why we can say, with confidence, that we know God *and* that we know God will always love us. Because God has acted lovingly toward us, and because we believe God always acts in ways consistent with who God is, we *know* that God is love (see 1 John 4:16). And because we know God is love and believe God always acts in ways consistent with who God is, we trust that the God who has loved us still loves us and will always love us. So we preach, and teach, and testify, and search for evidence of God's love, as Christian believers, even when the circumstances in which we find ourselves, and the ambiguities that surround us, seem to argue to the contrary.

The Scandal of Love Incarnate

The biblical witness consistently argues that our participation in the steadfast, boundless love of God on which we rely precipitates loving works that serve to promote social righteousness. David, in the prayer of confession he offers in Psalm 51, yearns to be healed by way of God's steadfast love that he might again show transgressors their ways and sing of God's righteousness (see Psalm 51:2, 13–14). He is convinced that God does not desire that he offer sacrifices as means to regain God's affection (see v. 16), but also that the offering of sacrifices will indeed follow renewed cognizance of his fellowship with God (see vv. 12, 19). He anticipates that God will both restore in him the joy of God's salvation and sustain in him a willing (or generous) spirit in such a way that he will be empowered to serve others in the context of that embrace.

Jesus, when he pays a visit to Peter just after his resurrection, insists that Peter's service to others flow from his love for Christ. Service to others cannot even be conceptualized, in John 21, apart from Jesus' relentless insistence on Peter's full participation in love. "Do you love me?" Jesus asks. He does not come to Peter merely to reassure him that he is loved, despite Peter's acts of betrayal. He comes to invite Peter's participation in the reality of this love. "Do you love me?" Jesus asks again. Those who have studied Greek, or those who have listened to pastors who have studied Greek preach on this passage, might remember that there is even more to Jesus' pushiness than a simple repeating of the question. For in this passage, more than one word for *love* is used. Jesus asks Peter, the first two times he questions him, whether Peter loves him with *agape*—the love of God so broad and long and wide and deep it "surpasses knowledge" (Ephesians 3:18–19). Each time, Peter responds by telling Jesus that he loves him with *fileo*—the love of siblings for one another. The third time, Jesus meets Peter right where he is, asking Peter if Peter loves him "like a brother" (*fileo*). Peter, no doubt relieved, answers: "Yes, Lord, you *know* that I *fileo* you!" But you can bet Jesus is back the next day, asking about *agape* again. And again.

Unlike Regis Philbin, the former host of the television game show *Who Wants to Be a Millionaire?*, Jesus isn't interested in receiving a final answer. This is because our participation in the love of God (our lives of discipleship) is not about giving the right or wrong answer and having the matter closed, one way or another. Participating in the love of God requires our submission to, and resubmission to, the loving God. The God who so loved the world that God entered in, in the person of Jesus Christ, and lifted us up. The God who looks us in the eye, with Peter, and asks us over and over again whether we love. The God who celebrates even our wading in love (*fileo*), but waits, and desires, our total immersion (*agape*).

It is in and out of participation in love that we engage that service that promotes social righteousness. "Do you love me?" Jesus asks. "Then feed my lambs and tend my sheep. Serve others not in obligation, but because they are my own, as you are. Promote social righteousness so that these lambs and sheep I love may live the abundant life (see John 10:10) I have promised."

Such love completely shatters everything we have known. We could have handled a perfectly righteous and holy God remaining at a distance from us. We could have come to worship, and striven to please, such a God. We could have accepted punishment, when we messed up, and offered gratitude, when we received blessings we did not deserve.

We also could have handled an omnipotent, perfectly righteous God who constructed a bridge between God and us. A God who became human to heal the rift caused by our sinfulness. A benevolent God who taught, and died, and rose to give us far more than we could ever deserve. A God who appeared to Peter to reassure him that God remains faithful even when we are not faithful. A God who, in the person of Jesus Christ, reaffirmed his love for Peter three times to somehow cancel out Peter's three acts of betrayal. We could have handled an incredibly benevolent, more than fair, loves-us-dopes-a-lot-and-therefore-inexplicably-looks-out-for-us kind of transactional God. God as the man in the yellow hat; we as Curious George. God as Alice Kramden (or Wilma Flintstone), and we as Ralph (or Fred). God as Ward (or June) Cleaver, and we as "the Beav." Yeah . . . we could have handled such a God, appreciated such a God, and even worshiped such a God.

What we can't handle is a God who enters fully into existence with us, looks us straight in the eye, and asks us if *we* love *God*. To answer this question in the affirmative is to enter into a level of commitment that might, in some ways, be harmful to certain forms of effective religiosity. It is to cease remaining awestruck and at a distance; it is to stop respectfully submitting to the terms of a "proper" relationship to God that we ourselves have conjured. It is to respond, when Jesus shakes us awake, by moving with him to the center of the Garden to kneel with him and pray. It is audaciously to lay claim to the identity that is ours in and through the One who has not only entered into existence with us, but lifted us into very existence with God's self. It is to know our exaltation, in and through this One whom God has highly exalted, as full participants in the life and work of God. To answer Jesus' question in the affirmative is to embrace Paul's charge to work out our own salvation with fear and trembling, precisely because it is God who is at work in us, enabling us both to will and to work for God's good purpose (see Philippians 2:12–13).

All God, and also us. *Also* us. Us really willing, really working, really contributing. Fully included in the divine life and work. Not contributing a little something—say, 56/100th of a percent to God's 99 and 44/100th percent. This is the miracle of love, that we are fully included. Fully. This is *your* address, and this is *your* house. "All that I have is yours . . . do *you* love *me?*"

It is no wonder that Eve and Adam, and also us, are overwhelmed. When we are considering their story, we focus almost solely on how they couldn't resist eating from the one tree that was out of bounds. It seems what they couldn't resist was finding a way to escape the fullness of the Garden, the pulsating freedom of it, the heavy sweetness of the fruit that required no toil, the safeness of the fields and forests in which there was no danger—no danger at all. No hunger, no killing, no brokenness—perfect communion.

That in which we find our freedom—the fount of superabundant blessings—also drowns us. By eating of the forbidden fruit, Eve and Adam found a way out. An escape from grace's clawing claim; a release from love's swallowing whole. To set up a workable economy—a transactional system that can "add love and stir" when it is convenient, but doesn't necessarily have to—is ever so much easier and more practical than understanding things, from the ground up, in accordance with love. To begin our lives, our relationships, and our work with love would change everything.

That is why we crucified Jesus. It was just too much for us to allow a person who lived and operated the way he did to stay around. His participation in God's grace, his reveling in God's love, caused too many problems for the system. And it causes too many problems for us, which is why we often tend to think about the event of the crucifixion as a kind of transaction, rather than a manifestation of God's grace-full posture to us, an indication of God's superabundant love. We accrued a debt, we explain, and Jesus paid it. Neat and clean and orderly and manageable, we chomp down on our apples and create

God in our own image, the transactional image of the world. And Christ looks down from that cross, with eyes full of the grace and love in which he participates, and says: "Father, forgive them; for they know not what they are doing" (Luke 23:34). He empties himself, entering into the depths of creaturely existence, to show us what it looks like to live into and out of the grace and love of God. We crucify him, replacing his testimony to God's unconditional love for the world with a "plan of salvation" that makes a whole lot more sense to us. One we can manage. One that is based on an economy of exchange, rather than on whom God has, and always has, revealed God's self to be.

One of the many difficult teachings of Jesus is the parable about the rich man and Lazarus in Luke 16:19–31. The rich man dies and goes to Hades; the poor man is on the other side of the chasm with Abraham. The rich man, in his suffering, begs Abraham to send Lazarus to warn his five brothers, so they might escape torment. "They have Moses and the prophets; they should listen to them," Abraham says. But the rich man does not think his relatives will pay attention to Moses and the prophets, so he suggests what he believes is a better plan. "If someone goes to them from the dead," he suggests, "they will repent." While this might seem like a good idea to us, Abraham can see right through it: "If they do not listen to Moses and the prophets," he says, "neither will they be convinced even if someone rises from the dead."

What Jesus did was not reveal a different God, but the same God who created all things good, inviting all to participate in the fullness of the gift. What Jesus did was direct our attention again to the God whom Moses and the prophets taught us relentlessly pursues us, the God whom we are commanded to love with all our heart, with all our soul, and with all our might (see Deuteronomy 6:5). You would think that the incarnation, the crucifixion, and the resurrection would get our attention and draw us back to the participatory existence that is God's creative and redemptive intention, an existence that cannot help but overflow in its abundance into the lives of others. "Do you love me?" this One asks. "Then feed my lambs. And tend my sheep." Jesus' question is, in truth, the question God has been asking us all along. When our answer is yes, Lazarus lives with a full stomach and the king with an understanding that a true sharing of life is a manifestation of genuine commitment to the other. It can never be precipitated from fear, obligation, or threat of punishment, but only by love itself.

The fact of the matter is that the level of commitment God insists we have is impossible to maintain. The *Shema* makes it sound so simple: Love God with all our heart, with all our soul, with all our might. *All* our heart? *All* our soul? *All* our might? Peter really gets it (for a change!) when he steps back from *agape* to *fileo*. And if on most days we cannot even act on the basis of *fileo,* we are still doing quite well to serve one another because we *should* (especially if occasionally, in the midst of our obligatory service, we experience "glimpses" of what it might look like to serve in utter freedom—*only* because we love).

If our limitations are one problem, when it comes to responding to God's question, our sin is another. The level of participation required is so great that it is hard for us to imagine, from this side of the Fall, how we could have established our individual identities. How could we have maintained a shameless, naked existence before God and one another without loss to who we are as unique individuals? How could we have sustained a "bone of bone, flesh of flesh" level of emotional connection without serving one another at our own expense? The so-called "sin" that violated the harmony of the created order could be interpreted, on this side of the Fall, as an act of self-protection or even self-discovery.

Love Incarnate in Community: Differentiated Selves, Responsible Selves
Paul Tillich and Harold Kushner, following up on such suspicions, have suggested that there's something necessary, and even good, about the Fall. Namely, it allows us to become autonomous, decision-making selves (even as selves who commonly make wrong decisions!).[20] While I think they are onto something important, in terms of complexifying the way we think about the human condition, I don't think they have it quite right. While we find a new identity in the Fall, it is clearly a shallow identity. It is an identity that is formed over and against participation, an identity that is individuated—at the expense of communion—for the purpose of more readily negotiating our relationships to God, to the earth, and to others.

In our fallen identities, we position ourselves to manage the consequences of the Fall, even if our managing involves covering ourselves with leaves and accepting our banishment from the Garden. We may be naked, we may be cast out, but at least we are not swallowed up by perfect fellowship with a God who walks with us and offers us everything God has. Much easier it is to finger point, and blame, and assign and accept penalties or praise. But in creating a manageable, differentiated identity we lose our created and redeemed identity. Our eating of the tree is more about our refusal to revel in all God has given us than about our taking of that which has not been offered. God's commandment not to eat of the one tree is not about removing a possibility *from* us, but about protecting us *for* the possibilities afforded by all of the other trees. To eat of the tree of the knowledge of good and evil is less about stealing something that doesn't belong to us than it is about rejecting who we truly are as those who are fully claimed and unconditionally loved.

Tillich and Kushner are right that we wouldn't be who we are without being differentiated from others. But insofar as we understand the differentiation of ourselves to be at the expense of our participation in the life of others (God, fellow creatures, creation), we are also not whom we were created and redeemed to be. If we are to advance the creative and redemptive will of God, we need to resist the common notion that individuation and participation are, in this world, fundamentally incompatible. While in this world (as Tillich very well describes it) there is constant conflict and negotiation between "individualization" and "participation," such conflict characterizes neither the creation (as such) nor the kingdom (as we are invited, by the work of Spirit through Scripture, to envision and promote it). I will return to imagining a nonconflictual kingdom in the following chapter. To lay the groundwork for this discussion, let me offer a brief but important theological reflection on how individuation and participation are *not* in conflict in the creation God identified as "very good."[21]

Consider the story of how human beings were created as it appears in Genesis 2:18–24. After finding no other animal suitable to be a helper and partner to Adam, God creates Eve out of Adam's side and brings her to him. While Adam undoubtedly recognizes Eve's difference from him, he does not respond to her as a competitor or some other kind of problem person he will have to work at negotiating a relationship with. He does not look her over and exclaim: "Since you are so different from me, you must be from another planet! I'm from Mars, you're from Venus,[22] and we'd better get some Deborah Tannen books so we can have a shot at communicating with one another."[23] Rather, Adam looks Eve right in the eyes, clearly amazed that he participates in this one who is so different, and that this one who is so different participates in him. "This at last is bone of my bones and flesh of my flesh!" he exclaims.

In this beautiful "pre-Fall" story, differentiation is not in conflict with participation. In fact, it serves to deepen it. Genesis 1:27, drawn from the earlier creation account, helps explain why this is the case. According to this text, God created human beings "in the image of God" as "male and female." As Christian believers, we understand that the God in whose image we are created is triune—one in three and three in one. Genesis 1:27, when interpreted with a Trinitarian lens in place, suggests that it is when human beings live in differentiated unity with one another that they reflect the image of the triune God who created them, the God who exists in differentiated unity with God's self.

Let me make this point again, perhaps more strongly. Genesis 1:27 explains that God creates Adam and Eve, *as male and female,* "in the image of God." As Christian believers, we confess that God is triune, that God is one in three and three in one. This means, in part, that there is no conflict between individuation and participation; between distinction and unity; between threeness and oneness; between the Father who is not the Son or the Spirit / the Spirit who is not the Father or the Son / the Son who is not the Father or the Spirit, and the God who is—always— all in all. When Adam was alone (only differentiated) it was "not good" (Genesis 2:18). When Adam joined with Eve, God looked over all God had made and deemed it "very good" (Genesis 1:31).

It is not individuation that is a problem, then. It is that we have claimed individuation at the expense of participation, or sacrificed individuation for the sake of participation, that is problematic. In fact, it might be that operating as though individuation and participation are necessarily at odds is our fundamental sin. To understand a divorce between the two as essential to the establishment of our freedom is to justify our sin, to give up on God's desire, to give up hope that the kingdom will come. To read Adam's joy-full "bone of my bones!" cry as romantic but impractical, and his "she made me do it!" accusation as painful but necessary for establishing his selfhood, is to have resisted grace, to have turned away from love. To assert, with self-righteous certainty, that we are not responsible for others— "Am I my brother's keeper?" (Genesis 4:9)—is to be completely and utterly lost.

To imagine the kingdom is to turn from all this and look directly into Jesus' eyes—to hear him asking us that question, again. There he is, asking us if we love him, refusing to settle for a negotiated relationship. He refuses to be merely a "bridge" between God and humanity, inviting us instead to recognize our full communion; confident that, in the context of this communion, the promotion of social righteousness will be a given.

To participate in such love is to be transformed. It is to become the new creations God desires us to be, willing and working for God's good purpose. It is to be exalted in and through the One who entered into existence with us and refused to leave us behind. This is the One who did not consider equality with God something to be grasped, the One who empties himself and takes the form of a servant, the One who obeys even unto death on the cross. And he keeps on asking Peter the question, and keeps demanding full participation—this One who continues to meet us where we are and invite us in. This Word-become-flesh, in the incarnation, held nothing back from us. Even when we betrayed him, he refused to resist arrest (see Matthew 26:53). This One who forgave us as he died (see Luke 23:34) descended even more deeply than death itself so he could be with and for us. He showed us there is no place where we can be safely lost, no place where we can escape the tyrannous pursuit of our Lover God.[24] "If I ascend to heaven, you are there; if I make my bed in Sheol, you are there. If I take the wings of the morning and settle at the farthest limits of the sea, even there your hand will lead me, and your right hand shall hold me fast" (Psalm 139:8–10).

When Cain asks if he is his brother's keeper, he has forgotten the radical presence of this God to whom he is speaking, a God near enough for the divine ear to hear Abel's blood crying out from the ground. When Adam accusingly declares that Eve made him do it, he spurns his inextricable connection both to the God in whose image he is made and the person with whom his existence in this image is made complete.

Neither Cain nor Adam served the lambs and sheep with whom they were in relationship, the lambs and sheep so loved by God, the lambs and sheep they would have loved had they not rejected their full inclusion in all God had made. Neither promoted social righteousness, nor created an environment in which their fellow beloved ones could flourish. What happened to the familial bond that joined Cain and Abel as siblings, as the first siblings on earth? What happened to Adam's exulting celebration of Eve as "bone of my bone and flesh of my flesh," as the first man and women ever to live? These basic human communities supposed the most readily to promote social righteousness seem to be the ones first to fail, the ones first to be broken, the ones first to turn away from the claims of love.

This might come as little surprise to us, given the character of sinful human existence, despite how utterly shocking and unacceptable it is. One of the times I remember what a shock brokenness is *supposed* to be is when I'm trying to explain to my three-year-old daughter and my five-year-old son why they need to be consistently on guard lest a "mean person" try to do them harm. It is clear whenever we have these discussions that they understand the earth to be a wonderful place full of wondrous people who are here to be celebrated and enjoyed. Their befuddlement at trying to understand how it could be that someone might try to do them harm reminds me to grieve the many ways the reality of our daily existence does not fit the reality of the kingdom—the many ways we, and those around us, refuse to acknowledge our participation in the love of God.

It has become common knowledge that most murderers and abusers know their victims and have often made explicit or implicit promises to love, protect, and/or nurture them in special ways. Husbands harm the wives they have pledged to love; parents hurt the children whose very existence is contingent on their ongoing care; friends abuse friends who have trusted them with hopes and confidences. Righteousness is *not* being promoted even, and *especially*, in these most basic of human communities. Perhaps this rampant abuse of one another by those who are supposed to love one another is some version of original sin, manifested systemically. Trying to make sense of the horror, we struggle to offer explanations about how hate isn't the "opposite" of love, but some twisted version of love gone awry. It is indifference, and not love, that is the opposite of hate, we say. Hate still manifests the same level of passion, the same level of investment.

However, hate and love are not the same things at all. Hate, and the abuses it breeds, is entirely alien to love and its fruits. There can be no meeting of unrighteousness with righteousness, injustice with justice, or unmercifulness with mercifulness. To have turned *toward* evil, succumbing to temptation, is to be in an altogether different place than to have been delivered *from* evil. The apostle Paul is rather direct about this in his letter to the church in Ephesus. To "live in love" (Ephesians 5:2), he says, is to live as those who "take no part in the unfruitful works of darkness, but instead expose them" (v. 11). Part of our work, as promoters of social righteousness, is to expose that which is antithetical to love, in the hope that it might be restored to God's creative and redemptive intentions.

Working Together: Promise, Grace, and Love

We have now discussed three bases for the work of promoting social righteousness. It will come as no surprise to anyone reading this book that the promise, grace, and love of God are related to one another. But how do they work together to support the promotion of social righteousness?

I propose that all three have something to do with restoration, or making whole. Clearly, the coming of the kingdom of God is about God's working in history to bring to fruition God's creative and redemptive intentions. It is to restore us, personally and corporately, to who we really are, as children of God. The point of our promoting social righteousness is to participate in God's restorative work on a corporate, as well as an individual, scale.

With this restoration matrix in place, the promise of God might be understood as a statement about the ultimate reality of the restoration that is not yet here but *is* a sure thing. As we have discussed, understanding the work of promoting social righteousness to be based in God's *promise* is to remember who we are as the children of "Our Father," impetuously laying claim to the restoration we believe is the reality. Along exactly these lines, theologians are fond of saying that "we live in the tension between the 'now' and the 'not yet' ": the "now" naming the certainty of God's promise to restore, which is such a sure thing that we claim it as a reality; the "not yet" naming the actual shape of our daily existence, which evidences all too consistently that the promised kingdom has not yet arrived.

While the promise of God throws us constantly into the joyous, dangerous quandary of living (Abram and Sarai-style) in relation to the impossible, the grace of God undergirds and enlivens us. As we watch, pray, and work for the promised restoration as those who refuse to give up on the "now" in the context of the "not yet," the grace of God continuously restores us. Even as we impatiently stomp our feet, recommitting ourselves to doing the work that will advance the coming of the kingdom, the God of grace is fully and actively engaged in the creative work of making us whole—forgiving us, drawing us back into relationship, reminding us of God's promises, turning us away from doubt and toward the impossible. The faith we manifest—as the promise-claiming, will-doing, Lord's Prayer-praying children of God—is itself the grace of God, running over and through us.

If the promise of God names the reality that gives our work purpose, and the grace of God names God's continuous undergirding—remaking of us even as we engage the tasks we are called to—the love of God names the character of the energy that fills us and enlivens us to work for restoration. When our work is founded in the love of God for us promoters of social righteousness, it is not done out of obligation, but in freedom. We serve others because we love them; in fact, our service is a concrete manifestation of our love, and our participation in the love of God. Like those sheep in Matthew 25, we hardly realize we have done anything at all.[25]

Perhaps some analogies will help here. Consider what happens when people make vows to one another. In a marriage ceremony, two people lay claim to God's promised reality of restoration. Consider the marvelous absurdity of it: the two "become one flesh" (Genesis 2:24). Then they go forward and commit themselves to establishing a small community that reflects the values of God's kingdom. In the years they spend together, if the relationship is one that works to realize wholeness, there is a continuous process of remaking and restoration—forgiveness, and brokenness, and renewal—that is energized by the love each partner in the marriage has for the other. One could say that a good marriage is a tiny community in which social righteousness is promoted: God's promise, God's grace, and God's love are the basis; justice, mercy, and humility are operative; bread, forgiveness, and freedom are in evidence.

This is the dynamic operative even in those relationships we are not apt to identify as loving. For example, as a teacher I have had the privilege of working with groups of students who covenant to do their part to develop an effective learning community in the classroom; live into the reality of grace that allows them to listen to, speak to, and critique one another; and submit to the love that is present. This love is the "energy" that drives the students'—and this little community's—continuous remaking and restoration. The love for one another that enlivens a good class is not the same kind of erotic love that forms a good marriage. Yet it is a love that is fully embodied. Students who are colleagues becoming also friends, or friends becoming also colleagues, or strangers coming to know *one another* as well as what is being said and taught, relate to one another as whole, physical beings. They lean forward to listen and speak; they laugh or scowl at the comments of others; they work to impress because they respect the opinions of the others.

Increasingly, in a developing classroom community, members manifest signs not only that they see the point of the course requirements listed on the syllabus (e.g., faithful attendance, preparation, participation), but that they *are* "with and for" one another, even if only for a twelve-week semester, in the context of this little, frail, power-full community. One could say that a strong class is a community in which members promote social righteousness in their relationships with one another. Promise and grace and love are just under the surface. Justice, mercy, and humility are operative. Bread, forgiveness, and freedom are in evidence. (In the most formed class communities I've had the privilege to teach, I mean this quite literally. As the course progresses, students suddenly start bringing and circulating homemade snacks, increasingly find ways to affirm and draw in those who initially appeared at the "fringe" of the class, and energetically plan ways to share what they are learning and experiencing with the other communities to which they are related.)

While we often set our sights for marriage far lower than I have here described it, and while it would be bogus to suggest that classroom experiences are generally characterized by the solidarity we teachers hope for and occasionally glimpse, there is a community that consistently and audaciously claims, as part and parcel of its identity, that it is a place where social righteousness is promoted. This community is the church.

Even in its worst moments, the church is a place that keeps sight of God's promises. Individuals may be overcome with doubt, but there will always be the biblical texts that remind us, a brother or sister who prays for us, and the Spirit who "intercedes with sighs too deep for words" (Romans 8:26). In the context of the body of Christ, the promises of God are always remembered—even when individual members forget.

In the context of the church, we claim the working of grace, the reality of our ongoing creation and restoration; our unmaking and our remaking into new creations (see 2 Corinthians 5:17); our conformation to the image of the Son (see Romans 8:29). Even when we give up on grace—reducing the impossible to something possible and achievable—even when we tragically switch to a more marketable, transactional way of speaking about the character of our relationship to God, the font is still there. The Table is there. We bump into them, and have to walk around them, as preachers and worship leaders. We have to get wet, or watch someone else get wet, at least occasionally. And we have to sit through an especially long service (which gets many of us a bit agitated!) every month or so. We dutifully chew, and we swallow, and we pray. And so, with these ordinary means something extraordinary happens: We are brought beyond the "practical" and the "realistic," even against our better judgment, and back into the order of grace that we (on our better days) claim is the real reality of our existence. We are restored, again. And we are then sent out into the world to work for restoration.

This is precisely where love spills over in works that promote social righteousness. Claiming the promise of God's love, restored by the working of grace to being who we are—in solidarity with one another—as God's beloved children, we go forth as those who love. Loving others, we serve them. We serve not out of obligation, but because we are with and for other people even as God is with and for us. We love others, in short, because God first loved us (see 1 John 4:19).

If to sin is to lose sight of our participation in love, to be restored is to remember, again, that we are full participants in God's unconditional love. It is to claim, again, the fullness of God's promise that God's kingdom will come and every stomach will be filled. It is to expect, again, that the gracious God will make the impossible possible and all will be forgiven. It is to recognize humbly that we who have little to recommend us as essential participants in the life and work are free to act, create, and live as partners in the ministry of reconciliation (see 2 Corinthians 5:18–20).

To have faith like children might mean letting go of some of our sophistication and wisdom about the "way things are" long enough to be shocked again. Shocked because we are living so closely in touch with the things of the kingdom that we recognize people being mean to one another as an extraordinary problem and not as an inevitable condition of our existence. Shocked out of love; shocked into action. To live as people of faith, to live so deeply in love, is to "have the power to comprehend, with all the saints, what is the breadth and length and height and depth, and to know the love of Christ that surpasses knowledge, so that [we] may be filled with all the fullness of God" (Ephesians 3:18–19).

Having cited this deep desire of Paul for his brothers and sisters at the church in Ephesus, I cannot help but close this chapter with his reminder to them, which comes exactly at the center of the letter and moves directly from a discussion of love into discussion of the character of Christian life. Paul writes: "Now to him who by the power at work within us is able to accomplish abundantly far more than all we can ask or imagine, to him be glory in the church and in Christ Jesus to all generations, forever and ever" (Ephesians 3:20–21).

Let us turn now to imagining that which is beyond anything we can imagine: a kingdom characterized by justice, mercy, and a humble walking with God.

Study Questions

1. Why is it important to ground the promotion of social righteousness in the promise, the grace, and the love of God?

2. What is God's most fundamental promise, and how do we go about claiming it?

3. Do you agree with the author that it is important that we recognize the "impossible" character of God's grace? Why or why not?

4. What is the relationship between God's unconditional love for us and our service to others?

Notes

1. By Jesus, who instructs us that this is how we should pray (see Matthew 6:9).
2. This is a paraphrase of John 10:9–11.
3. Karl Barth, *Church Dogmatics,* 13 vols. (Edinburgh: T. & T. Clark, 1958), Vol. IV/2, p. 307. Hereafter abbreviated as *"CD."*
4. My "giving the Holy Spirit a chance" is an act of faith that is itself part and parcel of the work of grace.
5. John Calvin, *Institutes of the Christian Religion,* 2 vols., ed. John T. McNeill (Louisville: Westminster John Knox Press, 1960), III.20.
6. See, for example, 1 Thessalonians 5.
7. Faith is, for Calvin, the "firm and certain knowledge of God's benevolence toward us, founded upon the truth of the freely given promise in Christ, both revealed to our minds and sealed upon our hearts through the Holy Spirit." *Institutes,* III.2.7.
8. *Institutes,* III.20.
9. *Institutes,* III.20.36.
10. *Institutes,* III.20.36. Calvin cites, in relation to this, Isaiah 49:15.
11. *Institutes,* III.20.36. Calvin cites, in relation to this, Matthew 7:11.
12. *Institutes,* III.20.37. Calvin is drawing from Luke 15, the parable of the prodigal son.
13. "A Brief Statement of Faith," from the *Book of Confessions,* Part I of *The Constitution of the Presbyterian Church (U.S.A.)* (Louisville: Office of the General Assembly, Presbyterian Church [U.S.A.], 2007), 10.1, line 1.
14. Dietrich Bonhoeffer, *The Cost of Discipleship* (New York: Touchstone, 1995).
15. "Amazing Grace" was written by John Newton and first published in Newton's *Olney Hymns* in 1779.
16. Marilynne Robinson, Pulitzer Prize-winning author of *Gilead,* describes this problem in the context of discussing Calvin, noting that it lies at the core of his theological system.
17. Søren Kierkegaard, *Fear and Trembling,* ed. Howard V. Hong and Edna H. Hong (Princeton: Princeton University Press, 1983), pp. 16–17.
18. I especially have in mind Richard Dawkins's bestselling book, *The God Delusion* (New York: Houghton Mifflin, 2006).
19. At this point, I am talking about why the doctrine of the Trinity matters to our lives of faith.

20. See Paul Tillich's *Systematic Theology,* vol. 2, and Harold Kushner's *How Good Do We Have to Be?*
21. This is in contrast to Tillich's and Kushner's views that the two are, necessarily, in conflict.
22. This is an allusion to John Gray's bestselling book series that begins with the title *Men Are from Mars, Women Are from Venus* (1992).
23. Deborah Tannen's books include *You're Wearing That?: Understanding Mothers and Daughters in Conversation* (2006), *You Just Don't Understand: Women and Men in Conversation* (1991), and *Talking from 9 to 5: Women and Men at Work* (1995).
24. I have in mind a sermon Tillich once preached on Psalm 139 titled "Escape from God." It can be found in *The Shaking of the Foundations* (New York: Charles Scribner's Sons, 1955).
25. This interpretation of the text I learned from William Greenway by way of an adult education class he taught several years ago at the University Presbyterian Church in Austin, Texas. It is foundational to my understanding of what the promotion of social righteousness *looks like* when it extends from our full participation in love.

Imagining the Kingdom: The *Shape* of Social Righteousness

3

I watch, as Alexander, four, and Jessica, two, prepare a meal on their play kitchen set. Alexander is the cook. He is frying an egg for Jessica. He breaks the egg into the frying pan, turns on the burner, and flips the egg over to cook both sides. He warns his sister, wide-eyed watcher, not to touch the stove, since it is hot and she might be burned. He carefully removes the egg from the pan and places it on a plate. "Don't eat it yet!" he warns Jessica, who weighs the seriousness of his words in exactly the same way she does when I give her a *real* egg, on a *real* plate. "You have to blow on it first," Alexander instructs.

Alexander and Jessica *imagine* cooking and giving, watching and receiving. Their imagining is the vehicle through which they participate in cooking and in giving, in watching and receiving. And their participation, precipitated by imagination, gives way to contribution. Hospitality is in evidence, every bit as much as when the eggs are real and the pan is hot. A little sister receives from the hand of her big brother; a big brother is permitted the joy of making a fried egg for his little sister; social righteousness is promoted. And the kingdom of God is brought a little closer to earth, as it is in heaven.

In the previous chapter we considered the *basis* for our work of promoting social righteousness. We emphasized that the work does not and cannot begin with *us,* but rather is grounded in God. We are impatient to witness the social righteousness that is indicative of the kingdom of God because God has promised us God's kingdom will come to earth as it is in heaven. The basis of our impatience is not our right, but God's promise. And the basis of any action we take to manifest God's kingdom in and to this world is the reality of God's unsurpassable grace and unconditional love. On the basis of our own efforts, we might be able to make the world a better place. But we won't be able to make lions lie down with lambs, or wipe every tear away from every eye, or ensure that every child in the world goes to bed every night with a full stomach. At best, we—in and of ourselves—can make a small difference. We can practice random acts of kindness and senseless beauty[1] that might in some small way touch the lives of others, but we will know better than to attempt to transform things at their core. When we focus on our own capacities, our best hope is that somehow God will take the limited things we are able to do and maximize their impact.

But when our work is founded in the promises of a grace-full and loving God, our focus is not on what we can and can't do, but on what God intends to do and on how God desires to work with us. While we (on our own) can only upgrade the possible, God (with us) makes the impossible possible. A stuttering man leads the chosen ones into the Promised Land; a virgin bears the Savior of the world; fishermen and peasant women receive the Spirit and become the Church. The grace-full, loving God makes possible the impossible dreams God has promised. And this God includes us in bringing these possible impossibilities to fruition. As God used Moses, Abram, and Sarai, as God used Mary, Peter, and Paul—so God uses us. Essentially. Irreplaceably. We who can do nothing, in and of ourselves, are fully included in the divine life and work. We can do more than tweak, more than improve, more than contribute a little something that we hope, somehow, will make a small difference. Rather, we can engage the bold work of promoting social righteousness because we have faith that we who can do nothing in and of ourselves can do all things in him who strengthens us (see Philippians 4:13).

With this reminder in play, we move in this chapter from reflection on the basis for the kingdom to consideration of the kingdom's shape. To make this move takes some imaginative effort. This is because the kingdom is not something realistic or self-evident. It is fundamentally impractical, defying the realities of our daily existence. It represents not simply a tweaking of this world, but a world that is altogether different from everything we know.

Thy Will Be Done

If the previous chapter is grounded in the demand we make, every time we pray the Lord's Prayer, that "God's kingdom come!" this chapter finds its locus in the line that directly follows: "thy will be done." All of us probably agree that it is harder both to know and to live according to God's will than we might have hoped. Most Christian believers have asked, on more than one occasion, "How do I know what God's will is?" Consistent with the emphases in the prior chapter, the basic answer to this question assumed here is: "We know what God's will is when and insofar as we participate in the desire of our gracious, loving God to bring God's kingdom to earth as it is in heaven." Well. That makes it sound relatively simple. Except, of course, that we know it is not. "But how, exactly, do we participate in the desire of God?" we ask. "How do we participate so deeply and freely in the life and work of God that our doing of God's will is simply an extension of our participation?"

One way we do God's will as an extension of our participation is to *imagine* what God's kingdom is like—to imagine what God desires. In the context of our imagining the kingdom God desires, the Holy Spirit forms us into doers of God's will. In short, our imagination serves as a vehicle through which the Spirit works to facilitate our participation in the promises, grace, and love of God in such a way that God's desires become our desires, and our desires break forth into concrete actions that advance the coming of the kingdom. In the first two verses of Romans 12, Paul exhorts us to present our bodies as living sacrifices, to resist being conformed to the world, and to be transformed by the renewing of our minds. Here we see imagination in play. Through imagining the kingdom of God ("setting our minds on things above"; Colossians 3:2), our minds are renewed. And at this point, precisely, we "discern what is the will of God—what is good and acceptable and perfect" (Romans 12:1–2).

Arguments against Imagination

Talk of "imagination" will raise some suspicions. First, we might understandably say, doesn't imagination concern itself with the "not real"? The last thing we, as promoters of social righteousness, want to do is portray the kingdom of God as a nice idea, an inspiring metaphor, but not something that will actually come to be. Too often, in the history of Christendom, eschatological[2] concepts have been misused to establish not-real, imaginary worlds in which people can escape from the painful realities of the "real" world.[3]

The kind of imagining I have in mind, unlike the kind Christopher Robin engages until he is six (when he becomes too old for such frivolity), is not devoted to creating worlds that will not, and do not, exist. The kingdom of God is not an imaginary place in which not-real, talking animals get stuck in honey pots, rescue each other from the "rain rain rain" that comes "down down down," or make last-minute plans for birthday parties. The kind of imagining I have in mind is not the kind we should grow out of as we become more conscious of, and responsible for, the realities of this world. Of course, too often we do grow out of it, as our exposure to the world's atrocities render us increasingly hope-less and cynical. But this is a bad thing, we hold, as people of faith. And so we work, at the Table, to revive our imagining; to recapture the kingdom we claim is real; to remember our real home is characterized by all receiving bread, and all living in reconciled relationship, and none succumbing to temptation. While such imagining is surely as far-fetched as imagining Winnie-the-Pooh and the Hundred Acre Wood, it is grounded in the promises, grace, and love of God and not in our own wishes and desires. This imagination participates in the reality of God rather than advancing our own projected realities.

We might have a second, related objection to thinking of promoting social righteousness in terms of *imagination*. In short, we are worried that imagining the kingdom of God will lead to the creation of idols. What is to prevent our imaginations from running amok, from leading us to desire and construct worlds of our own making, rather than God's making? What is to ensure our imaginations don't pull us away from the reality of the kingdom of God, as God has established it, toward trumped-up versions of kingdoms of this world? Certainly, a quick survey of history uncovers example after example of earthy kingdoms formed through the exercise of imagination. Some of these kingdoms have preserved and advanced life as much as possible, but not completely; most have expended the lives of the less powerful to benefit those of the more powerful; none are the kingdom of God in which *all* share fully, and equally, in life.

What ensures our imaginations lead us not to create kingdoms of this world, but rather to contribute to the real reality of the kingdom of God, is attentiveness to starting point. Our starting point for imagining is not first and foremost what *we* desire, but what *God* desires. What we imagine is not the fabulous kingdom that would be possible *if* this world granted us more resources and certain superpowers. We imagine, rather, the kingdom that is not of this world because it is ruled by a God who is *totaliter aliter* ("totally other"). We imagine that which is beyond anything we can imagine, because the kingdom belongs to the One who "by the power at work within us is able to accomplish abundantly far more than all we can ask or imagine" (Ephesians 3:20). The imagining I am talking about here is founded in relationship to that One who has claimed us as God's children: the One who makes outlandish promises, the One who continuously remakes and restores us, the One whose love is poured out and into us so fully that it spills over into works of love.

Faithful Imagining: Proclaiming the Majesty of God

Calvin, I believe, had precisely this kind of imagining in mind when he instructed people of faith to proclaim the majesty of God. He thought this should be the agenda of every sermon, of every Christian education class, and of every confession of faith we make in the context of private conversations. When speaking with members of the "visible church" (those who know their election in Jesus Christ)—*proclaim the majesty of God*. When speaking with those who might well be participants in the "invisible church" (those who are not yet cognizant of their election)—*proclaim the majesty of God*. We are called to proclaim the majesty of God, according to Calvin, both to edify the established Christian community and to evangelize those who might one day become members of it. As we bear witness to God's majesty, the Holy Spirit draws hearers more deeply into participation in the life and work of God.

In proclaiming the majesty of God, Calvin employs imagination. He does not imagine his way from himself to God. Rather, he begins with God's self-revelation, contemplating God's acts playfully and joyously. Contrary to the usual stereotypes, Calvin writes about God's actions on our behalf as though he is a kid in a candy store. He insists, for example, that "there is not one little blade of grass, there is no color in this world that is not intended to make [us] rejoice"[4] and that therefore we are "not only to be spectators in this beautiful theater but to enjoy the vast bounty and variety of good things which are displayed to us in it."[5] Reveling in the marvelous reality of God's self-revelation, he watches a nurse speaking tenderly to the baby in her charge and imagines God as our loving caretaker, lisping to us.[6] Testifying to the fact that there is distinction but not division in the life of the triune God, he cites the beautiful words of Gregory of Nazianzus: "I cannot think on the one without quickly being encircled by the splendor of the three; nor can I discern the three without being straightway carried back to the one."[7] In these three quotes alone we witness Calvin bursting with imagination as he celebrates the things of God.

Calvin's creative proclamation of the divine majesty is, I believe, grounded in his conscious participation in the life of the God who makes promises, the God who claims us by grace, and the God who empowers us through love. In other words, his imaginative language is not one strategic element in a system he employs to be a more winsome theologian or a more effective preacher. I'm certain he does not have, stacked on the corner of his desk, a pile of books instructing him on how to use catchy, marketable language to captivate one's congregation or audience.[8]

Whatever is piled on the corner of his desk, one thing is clear: Calvin's imaginative language at the same time extends from and bears witness to his participation in the life and work of God. Calvin proclaims the majesty of God as one who reflects habitually on his relationship with God; in the context of his life of prayer he imagines what God desires, both for himself and for this world. And he comes to participate ever more deeply in it, in such a way that God's desires, by the power of the Spirit at work within him, continuously form—and correct—his own.

Calvin's participation in the work and will of God, facilitated by such imagining, then gives way to world-changing action. Submitting to the exhortations of a Christian brother,[9] he tears himself away from his safe circumstances and goes to Geneva; he writes the *Institutes* and the treatises of the Reformation; his prose contributes to the shaping of modern French. He supports separation of church and state[10] and advocates for more humane methods of criminal punishment.[11] He makes such strong provision for education that his vision extends to the western world. Concerned to minimize the possibility of disease in the city of Geneva, he is also largely responsible for the installation of a closed sewer system.[12] All these things Calvin accomplishes, it seems, with an eye toward the coming kingdom of God, never forgetting (as we discussed in Chapter 1) that "grace alone brings about every good work in us."[13]

The Kingdom of Heaven Is Like . . .

If Calvin's example of how to promote social righteousness without wavering one iota from a God-centered theology isn't enough to license the use of our imagination, consider the example of Jesus. Jesus has the habit of using whatever is at hand to proclaim the majesty of God, inviting others to participate so fully in it that their participation contributes to its coming. Jesus encourages a Samaritan woman to deepen her faith by referencing something she needs, and carries, every day—a bucket of water (see John 4). The woman begins to *imagine* never having to draw or to drink. Jesus invites a religious leader named Nicodemus to think of spiritual renewal in terms of the everyday occurrence of childbirth.

Nicodemus begins *imagining* what it would be like to be born (see John 3). Jesus challenges the disciples to feed those who are hungry with what is at hand (see Matthew 14:13–21; Mark 6:30–42; Luke 9:12–17; John 6:1–14). He calls them to *imagine* that the contents of the lunch box of one little boy can feed all those people.

We know that the Samaritan woman is a good imaginer and that her capacity to trust Jesus (to imagine and to believe that what he was saying was true) leads her, in turn, to proclaim the good news to her townspeople. Unrelenting in her insistence that they "come and see" this one who tells her everything she has ever done (see John 4:29), the townspeople finally give in, eventually testifying that they have come to believe because they have met him for themselves (see v. 42).

Nicodemus and the disciples do not appear as able as the Samaritan woman to imagine the kingdom in which Jesus invites them to participate. "Can one enter a second time into the mother's womb and be born?" Nicodemus asks (John 3:4). He and Jesus part ways, on the night they have this conversation, with Nicodemus appearing still to be deeply skeptical. But he goes on to make two additional appearances in the Gospel of John, both which indicate he is stepping out of the kingdoms of this world and into the kingdom of God. First, in chapter 7, he reminds his fellow Pharisees and the temple police that Jewish law "does not judge people without first giving them a hearing to find out what they are doing" (v. 51). Second, in chapter 19, he assists Joseph of Arimathea in removing Jesus' body from the cross, embalming it, and burying it in Joseph's newly hewn tomb. Joseph, it seems, provided the tomb and the linen. Nicodemus, for his part, provided the spices—one hundred pounds of myrrh and aloe. Like Mary before him (see Mark 14:1–9), his gift is excessive. Because Nicodemus (alongside Joseph) is able to imagine a different reality than the one in which Jesus is nailed to the cross, Jesus' body is not left on the cross to decay, but is taken down and treated respectfully.

Like Nicodemus, the disciples find it difficult to imagine that God's desire for the people surrounding them might be realized. Concerned that the time for the evening meal is drawing nigh, they urge Jesus to recommend they break for the evening so that individual families can go into town and buy food for themselves. They recognize they do not have the resources to feed such a large crowd of people—in one Gospel, they note it would take six months' salary to buy enough bread for every person to have just a taste. But Jesus insists the disciples find a way to host the people. While each of the Gospel accounts suggests the disciples receive Jesus' plan with skepticism, they in no evident way resist his concrete instructions. They collect the bread and the fish, they organize the people into picnic groups, and they have enough faith not to turn on their heels and walk away from the scene, scandalized by the absurdity of it all. They have enough faith, it seems, to begin imagining what they clearly know is unimaginable.

Each of these figures in different ways promotes social righteousness. The Samaritan woman imagines the living water Jesus tells her about, and is drawn through the work of the Spirit into deeper participation in the life of God. Her imagining gives way to action: She goes back to her town and does the work of an evangelist, insisting her townspeople "come and see" this one she has met (see John 4:29) so they might enter into relationship to him and join in the fellowship of the kingdom. Interestingly, the passage makes a big point of telling us that the townspeople are moved to trek to the well and meet Jesus specifically by the woman's compelling testimony. "He told me everything I have ever done," she says (v. 39). Clearly, not only is this woman good at accepting Jesus' invitation to imagine; she is gifted at inviting others to imagine with her. "Could this be the Messiah?" she asks. She draws them in; they can't resist; they go to the well; they meet Jesus; and *then* they come to believe because they have met him for themselves (see v. 42).

Nicodemus continues to reflect on what Jesus has told him; the imaginative "born again" imagery is used by the Holy Spirit to draw him even more deeply into relationship to God through his relationship to Jesus. I like to think that Nicodemus's ongoing engagement with the beautiful and truth-full metaphor of Jesus gives way, finally, to his participation in the work of the kingdom. His giving of the spices and participation in the embalming and burial certainly serve to promote social righteousness on at least three levels. First, he who is presumably well off financially shares his wealth with Jesus, a man who is economically poor. He cares for the Good Teacher whom many dearly loved, the teacher through whom he comes to participate in life eternal. In providing for the care of Jesus' body, he participates in Jesus' ministry to bodies that thirst, and hunger, and groan for the completion of their redemption. In caring for Jesus, Nicodemus makes a contribution to the coming of the kingdom. He quite literally tends the body that will rise on Sunday, walk and talk and eat with the disciples, ascend to heaven to sit on the right hand of the Father, and come to take us to himself (see John 14). In caring for Jesus' body, Nicodemus is participating in the resurrection that has not even happened yet. He is living into, and thereby advancing, the new life Jesus has told him about. I like to imagine Nicodemus's joy at being born again on that Sunday morning and again at Pentecost.

And then there are those concerned, practical, initially unimaginative disciples. I try to fathom what must be running through their heads as they hand Jesus the five loaves and two fishes. They probably expect him to shake his head, woefully, as he agrees with them that it is time to bring the evening to a close. Instead, Jesus instructs them to have the people sit down for a meal. Clearly, something shifts in the disciples when Jesus gives them this instruction. Something moves them from "obviously *we* can't feed them" to "let's all sit down now and get ready to eat." You simply have to bolster some degree of imagination if you are going to have the guts to organize five thousand-plus people for a meal that is, for all intents and purposes, nonexistent. You must have some hope that this man who has been healing bodies and teaching bodies can also feed bodies out of nothing. To have such hope is, at the very least, to have the kingdom in sight—to glimpse the wedding table of the Lamb around which all are gathered, at which all are fed, at which none go hungry. And the disciples clearly help Jesus bring this kingdom to earth, as it is in heaven, with their organizing and collecting. In their imagining, which enables them to participate, they contribute to bringing the kingdom into being.

Imagining the Kingdom: Micah 6:8

In the remainder of this chapter, I turn to consideration of what the kingdom of God *looks like* when we submit to the Spirit in imagining it. And how, exactly, do we step into what we imagine, "doing the justice" and "loving the mercy" indicative of the kingdom even as we "walk humbly with our God"? Here is a beginning answer to these questions, which the remainder of this book will go on to develop:

In imagining what God promises us, God's creative and redemptive desires become our own. We begin desiring what God desires . . .

> . . . We imagine a kingdom characterized by God's promised justice; we witness the beauty of justice; we desire for justice to be the reality of our existence; we begin living justly; we thereby do justice.

> . . . We imagine a kingdom regulated by God's grace; we experience the freedom afforded by grace; we desire for grace to be the rule rather than the exception; we begin living mercifully; we come to love mercy.

. . . We imagine a kingdom resplendent with love; we know what it is to be wholly overtaken by love's claim; we want all to know the joy of being loved regardless of any degree of deservingness or undeservingness; we begin loving as God loves; we walk with humility.

Let us look at each of these in more detail.

Doing Justice

According to Micah 6:8, the Lord requires three things of us: to do justice, to love mercy, and to walk humbly with our God. To do the will of God is to do these things.

The Bible has a way of stating the most difficult things in a way that makes them sound overly simple. You can be reading along, feeling semispiritual and centered, and all of a sudden find yourself nodding in agreement before a passage like Matthew 22:34–40. *All we have to do is love the Lord our God with everything we've got, and love our neighbors as ourselves,* we might paraphrase to ourselves. *Yeah, I should be able to do that,* we may very well think. Or we read Micah 6:8, which doesn't seem to be bogged down by all those Levitical codes and doesn't say a thing, even, about the Ten Commandments, and we are lured into thinking: *Yes. Now that's reasonable. All we have to do is do justice, love mercy, and walk humbly with our God. All right, then.*

Then we start imagining what justice, love, and humble walking look like, and things get more complicated. In our imagining we begin to participate in the kingdom, where everything looks different from what we have ever known. When we submit to the will of the One who promises us, and graces us, and loves us, our own wills are changed. When we share in the desire of God that the kingdom come to earth as it is in heaven, God's desire becomes our own.

To do justice, love mercy, and walk humbly with our God is not only to join a new reality. It is to be ourselves completely unmade and remade—to become the new creations we are in Christ (see 2 Corinthians 5:17). Similarly, to do what God requires is not merely to take on a few extra responsibilities, but to live completely different lives.

When we start realizing this we might cease nodding emphatically and become a little concerned. Because if there's one thing we generally do not like, it's qualitative change to *ourselves.* Changes to others are OK, as long as they don't affect us too much. Changes to our circumstances are fine, as long as they add to what we think is good and take away from what we think is not. *Improvements* to ourselves are welcome, as long as they don't fundamentally change us.

Imagining justice is a threatening prospect because such imagining ultimately insists on actual participation and contribution. And to contribute by "doing justice" probably requires us to become different people than who we are right now. Imagining justice is particularly threatening to we who are wealthy—we who have economic, educational, technological, medical, legal, and other resources most others in the world do not have. This is because to imagine justice is to envision everyone having what they need, and to move from imagining justice to participating in it so deeply that we make a contribution *to* it requires fundamental change not only to how we handle our material resources, but also to who we are.

At precisely this juncture, we have a choice. We can choose to be unimaginative, fold up our arms, and view any talk of justice that involves us radically altering ourselves—and the way we utilize and share resources—as out of bounds. Or we can choose to imagine what Amos means when he talks about letting justice "roll down like waters, and righteousness like an ever-flowing stream" (Amos 5:24). It will come as no surprise to the reader that this book recommends imagining with Amos. But we need to be honest that such imagining involves real risks to ourselves, understanding that the Spirit might well use it to continue bringing God's work in us "to completion" (Philippians 1:6), as Paul writes to the church at Philippi, "so that in the day of Christ [we] may be pure and blameless, having produced the harvest of righteousness that comes through Jesus Christ for the glory and praise of God" (vv. 10–11).

Paul minces no words about the risk of participating in the kingdom. Shortly after his exhortation to the Philippians, he imagines the self-emptying and exaltation of Jesus Christ by way of a beautiful hymn (see Philippians 2:5–11). Directly following this extraordinary evocation, and assuming our participation in the reality in which it participates, Paul returns to his emphasis on our transformation: "Therefore . . . ," he writes, "work out your own salvation with fear and trembling; for it is God who is at work in you, enabling you both to will and to work for God's good pleasure" (vv. 12–13). The question is: Are we willing to live with the fear and trembling that comes with the cognizance that God is at work in us and that we are at work with God?

I was once mildly chastised, following a lecture I had given, for not clarifying that the "fear" Paul mentions in verse 12 has nothing to do with being afraid. Since this criticism seemed to make a good deal of sense, I found myself nodding emphatically, agreeing with the woman who explained that *fear,* in the context of this verse, should be translated as *awe.* "Fear," she said, "has nothing to do with our relationship to God, who does not want us to be afraid."

While I still agree with the woman that imagining God's promises to us in the event of Jesus Christ inspires awe, and I certainly concur that God does not want us to be afraid of *God,* I have come to suspect that being afraid might well be part of the equation when it comes to working out our salvation. While we should not be afraid of the God who has reached down to us and lifted us up, it makes sense to be afraid of the change that comes with living in relationship to this God. As we have discussed, we fear the change that comes with working out our salvation. Paul acknowledges this on the way to exhorting us to keep working on it: We might be afraid, we might even tremble, but we'd better continue working it out. Keep your eye on the prize, Paul urges. Press on for that day of Jesus Christ (see Philippians 3:14).

Imagining Justice: Amos 5

There is nothing like reading some verses of Scripture in context to ignite both our imaginations and our fear. Amos 5:24 is one of those verses. It is breathtakingly beautiful, when we pause to contemplate it. Who has leaned over a railing and stared safely into a powerful waterfall without becoming aware of the glorious indifference of nature? The water pours down whether we are there or not; it will pour down whether we step under it or not; it will pour down after we are dead. It will roar as it pours and sparkle in the sun as it brings with it, by the sheer force of gravity, anything that enters its path.

Who has camped by a mountain stream overflowing with melted snow unaware, in their sleep, of the splash of water against the rocks? The water twists and turns and growls and chatters when we are drinking our cocoa by the evening fire, and through the night that is sleepless or the night of deepest peace and rest. It cares not that we are there, but cradles us nonetheless. Because it does not need our presence, its inclusion of us is pure gift. Because it does not need our presence, being present to it is our choice, our opportunity, our risk.

The waterfall and the stream are there in the center of Amos, at the end of chapter 5. They are flanked by jolting portrayals of God *ridiculing* our "desire [for] the day of the Lord" (vv. 18–23) and *mocking* our belated efforts to be righteous (see vv. 25–27). The images of justice rolling down and righteousness flowing are set in contrast to the hypocrisy of our solemnity, our sacrifices, and our singing. The piety of the Israelites is also our piety: a spiritual showiness founded in the presumption of inclusion rather than reliance on God's promises, the religiosity of we who have trampled on the poor and taxed them unjustly (v. 11). "Why do you want the day of the Lord?" we are asked. "It is darkness, not light; as if someone fled from a lion, and was met by a bear; or went into the house and rested a hand against the wall, and was bitten by a snake" (vv. 18–19).

This imagery is terrifying. It is reminiscent of a horror movie, where a person runs from one dangerous figure into the arms of another. It reflects what we have feared, about nature, ever since the Fall—that it will overtake us, that it will destroy us.

Most disarmingly, those who will meet the bear and the snake are entirely oblivious to their fate. The text implies they are expecting something good to happen; that they *imagine* themselves stomping their feet and claiming God's promises; that they are gathering for worship, and fulfilling their pledges, and singing with gusto. It is these who will wail, these who will say "alas" (vv. 16–17). Like the goats in the Great Judgment scene, they will be stunned and confused when they are not permitted to enter, especially since they are good at saying "Lord, Lord," believing themselves to be sincere (see Matthew 25).

Who are these people? Are they someone else? Are they ever us? Are they never the poor, and always the rich?

Despite the confusion of the goats in Matthew 25 and those who "desire the day of the Lord" in Amos 5, the texts make it clear who should beware: Those who have not fed the hungry, clothed the naked, or visited the sick and imprisoned. It is those who "turn justice to wormwood,[14] and bring righteousness to the ground" (Amos 5:7), those who "hate" accurate judgments and "abhor the one who speaks the truth" (v. 10), those who "trample on the poor and take from them levies of grain" (v. 11), and those who "afflict the righteous . . . take a bribe, and push aside the needy in the gate" (v. 12). While there are a lot of verses in these texts identifying who is being condemned, they do not represent a long list of devastating sins. Rather, they all iterate manifestations of a single, unacceptable violation—justice has been compromised. The lives of some have been expended or neglected, ostensibly to benefit the lives of others. Making matters all the worse, those who have experienced marginalization are now using others for the sake of their own gain.

Who these people are is clear in the text. What we witness, in the shock of those who are bitten by snakes and the surprise of the goats that are not admitted to the kingdom, is not in the manipulative spirit of hyper-Calvinism. In other words, it is not the case that the Israelites, and the goats, and possibly we ourselves have done our level best to discern the will of God and to act in faithful accordance with it, but will someday nonetheless be "trumped" by a sovereign God who has foreordained, from the start, that we will remain on the outside. It is not the case that claiming God's promise that we are fully included in the kingdom is pointless, since God's promise may or may not have been made to us.

Rather, what the text tells us is that living in accordance with a kingdom of our own making, rather than the kingdom of God as it has been revealed, will get us into big trouble. It will get us into trouble regardless of how sincerely and faithfully we convince ourselves we are living. Our surprise, on that Day, will have nothing to do with God playing us and everything to do with our coming to the sickening recognition that we have been playing God, and that God has known all along.

For God's will, in its most crucial respects, is perfectly clear. It is not simple, but it is clear. It is *always* to be just: to take care of one another, to do what is right. God's judgment is *always* for the underdog: for the poor, for the hungry, for the sick, for the sinner.[15] God's command, which takes many forms, is, in the words of Karl Barth:

> self-evidently and in all circumstances a call for counter-movements on behalf of humanity and against its denial in any form, and therefore a call for the championing of the weak against every kind of encroachment on the part of the strong.[16]

The kingdom of God is *always* about the flourishing of *all* life, and never about the expenditure of some lives for the sake of enhancing the lives of others. The waterfall of justice is falling; the streams of righteousness are flowing; at the center of the City of God, all who thirst for the fullness of God's will are eternally quenched.

It is clear what we are to do; it is clear what God has promised. And yet we do not do it; we do not live in accordance with the promise. One reason we do not, in my observation, is that we mistake what seems to be necessary with what is right. We find ways to justify hating the truth-tellers, taxing the poor, and taking bribes when we believe it necessary to do so for the sake of preserving ourselves and/or our institutions. We might convince ourselves that we are being brave—doing what "needs to be done" from the vantage point of our relative positions of power, even though we would rather not do them. Feeling this way, we might enter into our solemn assemblies, and give our offerings, and sing up a storm to delude ourselves into believing we are still on the inside of the kingdom. Perhaps we yearn for the kingdom to come, in part so we can stop living the lie we don't fully realize we're living: the lie that privileges what is necessary over what is right, the lie that leverages the realistic against the impossible, the lie that lays aside God's promises of never-ending abundance for worldly promises that we can have a bigger share (for ourselves, our loved ones, our ministries, or our generally well-meaning institutions) if we only make the necessary sacrifice of taking from others.

If this describes us, Amos says, then darkness (and bears, and snakes) awaits us. Unless, that is, we change our ways and claim the promise of the water. "Hate evil and love good, and establish justice in the gate," we are advised (Amos 5:15).

But can we do this? Most of us who are caught in the hypocrisy of mistaking our own constructed piety for authentic faithfulness will respond by thinking to ourselves: *Whoever wrote this just doesn't understand how complicated it all is.* Of course, it's complicated. It's complicated to think we believe something and act in ways that are utterly antithetical to it: going to our assemblies, and giving our offerings, and singing our praises, while diminishing the lives of others. Hypocrisy is not only complicating, it is also exhausting. *Everyone* is weary, in our culture. So consistently are we weary that some of us have given up on getting enough rest in favor of wearing our weariness as a badge of honor. A colleague told me just the other day that he had "trained" himself to get by on five hours' sleep each night. "You get used to it," he assured me.

There are all kinds of reasons for being weary, the most obvious being that we work too hard. Another is that our anxiety drains us: because of the pressures to get our share or because our share is less than we had banked on. But I suggest there is another reason we are weary—particularly we who self-identify as Christian. I think we are weary because we are suffering the emotional drain that comes with living as unknowing hypocrites. We *think* we believe that loving God and neighbor is the most important thing. (What reader of this book *wouldn't* sign on, if asked, as a supporter of justice?) But we engage the politics of the workplace, and make many of our major life decisions, in a different mode altogether. In contrast to those promoters of social righteousness who coined the "WWJD?" question, we are leaving what Jesus would do up to Jesus and doing whatever it is that we figure we have to do for ourselves. Instead of striving to live "*in* the world but not of it," we are living "*of* the world but not in it."[17] Our values, when it comes to money management and political maneuvering, tend to reflect the values of culture. But, wanting to be spiritual, we gather in solemn assemblies, offer gifts, and sing songs of praise in ways that reinforce the perception (our own and possibly others') that we hover a bit above the nongathering folks, spirituality-wise.

It is no wonder we are worn out. We are living a double life, so committed to believing we are doing the right thing that we don't even realize the irresolvable contradiction. I think this is something the book of Amos is trying to shake us out of, when it sharply and disturbingly delineates what is going to happen, on "the day of the LORD," to those of us who have not done justice.

"But you don't understand," we might want to say back, "there is no other way." "There is no way except to continue in 'the feverish state of tension'[18] that is our way of life."

"If we think there is no other way," Barth once wrote, "we are always wrong." We are wrong, despite any "faithfulness, zeal, conscientiousness and good intentions" we may bring to our work, because "to work tensely . . . is to do so in self-exaltation and forgetfulness of God."[19]

While Barth is not, at this point, specifically discussing God's requirement to "do justice," he is observing that the will of God is never done when we have lost sight of the fact that all our work is done before God. Further, he makes the startling comment that "all our work is play" when done before the God who is sovereign. We are not called to figure it all out. We are called to be faithful. We are not called to do what appears to be necessary to keep the operation flowing. We are called to do what is right. We are not called to offer performances of our piety. We are called to do justice. We are called to engage the "serious play"[20] that is the play of the children of God. The play that imagines the world of "Our Father" and participates so creatively in enacting it that the kingdom of God is brought a little closer to earth, as it is in heaven.[21]

I Will Give You Living Water

In the middle of the darkness and the bears and the snakes, in the midst of the mockery of our ill-founded hopes and our hypocritical efforts, are the life-giving images of water. Rolling, falling, flowing, endlessly moving water. The water is what is respected. The water is what God wills. Not our festivals and not our "solemn assemblies." Not our offerings and not our songs. Not without the rush of water, anyway. Apart from the presence of justice and righteousness, these other things are unwanted. We who "trample on the poor" by "taking from them levies of grain" and those who take bribes or "push aside the needy in the gate" cannot compensate by attending more meetings at the church or singing more loudly each Sunday.

But we can do justice. We can return to what God is up to and join in. But first we need to recognize exactly where we stand in the narrative, rather than assuming we are on the inside (with the sheep and the poor!).

If we spend a little time contemplating the majesty of God, we might be able to see the waterfall of justice crashing down, the ever-flowing stream of righteousness gushing on around us. The water imagery evokes biblical stories about faith and the rewards of righteousness, about divine preservation and the flourishing of life. It evokes them at the same time it turns our easy interpretations of them inside out. It rains for forty days and forty nights, and God protects those living safely on the ark (see Genesis 6—9). *Can we continue to assume we are on the ark? Or are we among those who are drowning?* The Israelites walk between walls of water that have been parted by Moses under God's instruction (see Exodus 14—15). *Would we walk on the dry land? Or drown with the Egyptians?* Jesus, "to fulfill all righteousness," is baptized by John in the Jordan River (see Matthew 3:13–17). *If we join with him in that water, will we be driven with him, by the Spirit, into the wilderness?* The Samaritan woman drinks, and leads others to drink, the ever-flowing water that removes from them the constant burden of finding drink for themselves (see John 4). *Will we drink? Or are the burdens that define our existence and our value too dear to our hearts?* And in the middle of the City of God is "the river of the water of life, bright as crystal, flowing from the throne of God and of the Lamb," lined by fruit trees whose leaves "are for the healing of the nations" (Revelation 22:1–2). *This is the promise of God: that the water will finally offer life to us all, even if it drowns our sinful selves in the process.*

The flow of the waterfall of justice and the stream of righteousness is unending both in its abundance and its duration. Unlike anything we know in this world, the waters imaged here know nothing of the limits of space and time. Justice and righteousness, as they are portrayed in

Amos, are not quantifiable goods that need to be doled out generously but with prudence, taking into account the restrictions of this world. In this world there is a limit to how long a blindfolded Lady Justice can continue "weighing the evidence" in relation to any given case. For example, the U.S. Supreme Court recently determined that DNA testing cannot be considered a "right" of all prisoners, in part because—if it were to be—the rights of others to expeditious trials would be violated.[22] We simply do not have the resources in this world to turn over every possible stone. So numerous injustices are never resolved, and the more honest among us (and/or the most affected among us) live with this awareness.

To be people of faith is never to be satisfied with allowing the limits of space and time to delimit our understanding of justice as it is operative in the kingdom of God. It is to unreasonably insist that justice is not only for all, it is also for every. It is ever to weigh the new evidence, determined to ferret out even one who has been treated unjustly. It is not to push away the needy (see Amos 5:12b), but to give them one of our more-than-one coats (see Luke 3:11). It is to care about "doing justice" not for the sake of principle, but for the sake of people.

Doing Justice as Humanization

Paul Lehmann describes justice, along exactly these lines, as "humanization." To do the will of God as the promise-claiming children of God is to be in the business of making and keeping human life human.[23] Most theologians today would argue that Lehmann is too anthropocentric—that is, "human centered"—and that doing justice must involve reaching out to animals and the earth itself in addition to human beings. Consistent with this, they would agree wholeheartedly with Lehmann's core insight that the purpose of doing justice is to contribute to the flourishing of life as God intends it.

When doing justice is understood to be about promoting life rather than fulfilling obligations, it becomes apparent how it benefits the *doer* as well as the *receiver*. In Chapter 2 we discussed the importance of thinking of our relationship to God and to one another in participatory, rather than transactional, terms. To do justice, understood in the context of a participatory understanding, is to promote life by entering into life with the other so completely that sharing resources with them comes almost naturally—as an extension of our sharing of life. To give as freely as those unaware sheep give in Matthew 25. To give as God gives: not because we *have* to; not because we *should;* not because we are *obligated* to; not even because we have so much more than most others in this world that it simply makes sense. But to give because we are *for* and *with* these "others." To give because we share together with them in life. To give because, participating in the lives of these others, we come to love our neighbors as ourselves.

Doing Justice as Friendship

Gustavo Gutiérrez imagines doing justice, along these lines, as an extension of *friendship*. "Christ says, 'I do not call you servants, but friends,' "[24] he points out, going on to comment that:

> As Christians, we are called to reproduce this quality of friendship in our relationships with others. When we become friends with the poor, their presence leaves an indelible imprint on our lives, and we are much more likely to remain committed.[25]

The question that comes immediately to mind is: *How in the world am I supposed to "become friends with the poor"?* "The poor" seem to me either to live so far away, and/or to operate in such different social circles, that I have difficulty even imagining what such friendships would look like. *Why can't it be enough,* I whine (on some deeply frightened level), *simply to write a few more checks?*

In response to my knee-jerk reaction that friendship with the poor isn't possible for me, I imagine Gutiérrez patiently smiling, waiting for me to realize that my resistance is indicative of my sin, my unwillingness to take a risk for the sake of participation. I imagine my pastor friend, Sophie, sitting across from me, eating her lunch and listening with genuine sympathy as she scratches her flea-bitten ankles, bitten because her lunch just the day before was taken in the home of a person, living in east Austin, who could not afford to fumigate. I imagine friends from twenty years ago, when my husband and I lived in the Philippines, reading my comments about the impossibility of friendship and laughingly reminding me that *they* were my friends— remember? One of the many of these friends would be Sena, the woman who did our laundry. She figured out we were paying her more than we needed to and so set these "extra" funds aside, one day presenting us with two large handmade puppets. The materials could have bought her a couple of blouses, a few kilos of rice. But she presented us with those puppets—proudly, gratefully, believing in our friendship, participating in life with us, and showing us how to participate with her.

To imagine doing justice in the context of friendship is to imagine that any clear distinction between "givers" and "receivers" be finally dissolved. To imagine participating together in life is to envision those who have more (in the way of material resources) sharing their resources in ways that the givers gain as much as the receivers receive. To do justice is not for those of us who are richer to save or rescue those who are poorer; rather, it is for all of us to enter together into mutual self-giving.

There is an adage, usually cited by richer people who have realized a "rescue operation" mentality is ineffective, that says: "Give someone a fish and they eat for a day; teach them to fish and they eat for a lifetime." But this adage is not founded in the genuine participation of friendship. To befriend a person isn't necessarily to give a fish or to teach to fish (although either or both of these things might be part of it). To befriend is to sit down next to the person and join in the fishing, believing that they may fish better than we can, and to be open to the possibility that there may be reasons why they are hungry that have little to do with their fishing skills.

Can we imagine being so for and with one another that we no longer think of ourselves as the "givers" and others as "receivers"? It seems almost impossible to do so. Just as impossible, in fact, as imagining that we—the children of God—are privy to all God has (see Luke 15:31). Perhaps, when we have difficulty believing such things, we would do well to embrace the unimaginability of it all, remembering that God's promise, grace, and love—not our own understandings and efforts—are the bases of our hope.

Loving Mercy

How do we imagine a world characterized by mercy?[26] What would our lives and communities look like if we treated one another with compassion, with that tender compassion consistent with the depth of loving kindness the grace-full God has shown us?

When I was in labor with my first child, the doctor said: "OK, Cindy. Now, the next time you push, I want you to give it everything you've got *plus* a little bit more." And, of course, I managed to critique her statement (even in the midst of circumstances that were, well, not readily given to analysis!), thinking to myself: *Oh, c'mon, Karen. Give me a break. That statement doesn't even make sense. If I'm giving it everything I've got, there* isn't *a little bit more.* But I did what the doctor said, and Alexander was born shortly thereafter.

Do Justice, Love Mercy

Give it everything you've got, and then give a little bit more. Give everyone what they have earned, what they deserve, their fair share. And *also* give to those who have not earned, to those who do not deserve, to those who have no claim on any portion. Honor the paying of debts *and* forgive the debts that have not been paid. *Oh, c'mon already. Give me a break. What makes you think we've got all that to give?*

We don't, of course. Justice breaks the bank, and now this. This mercy we are called by God to love is founded in pure deficit, when it comes to our own resources. It is founded only, and completely, in the grace of God. The grace of God, as discussed in Chapter 1, is not commensurable with any system of exchange. It is, by any standard that we have, both impossible and absurd. While some might commend us for doing justice, we will more often be disrespected for loving mercy. While doing justice at least poses a threat to those who benefit from injustice, loving mercy—and acting in accordance with this love—takes us out of the dynamic of exchange altogether. To love mercy, and to demonstrate it, is to be a nonplayer in the system. It is at best to be overlooked and at worst (as we have said) to be seen a fool.

What does mercy look like? It looks like Cain, being marked for his protection rather than having his life taken, as a reasonable understanding of justice might demand. God acts justly; God acts mercifully. God does not overlook what has been done to Abel, *and* Cain's life is spared (see Genesis 4:1–15).

What does mercy look like? It looks like God's relationship to the Israelites, when provision is made for their salvation from death by snakes (see Numbers 21:4–9). They look upon the bronze snake, and they are protected. God acts justly; God acts mercifully. In the order of justice, God sends the snakes as punishment for the people's sin of speaking against God and Moses; in the order of mercy, God provides a way to escape the punishment.

What does mercy look like? It looks like Jesus, who judges the woman caught in an act of adultery but does not condemn her (see John 8:1–11). God acts justly; God acts mercifully. Acknowledging the truth of the law, Jesus exhorts the woman to sin no more. Realizing the purpose of the law, Jesus spares her life and sends her away from those trapped in conceptions of justice absent of mercy.

In these three examples, mercy clearly does not skip over justice, even though it is at the same time altogether different from it. It is a little hard to grasp how mercy respects justice even as it operates on a different plane.

Descriptively, the biblical examples presented above suggest that to love mercy is not to set justice to the side. Notice that God did not say, for example: "Oh, well, I guess I'll just forget about the killing of Abel so I can stay in relationship to Cain." Similarly, God never simply overlooks the disobedience of the Israelites; the unjust acts of God's forgiven people rarely escape consequences or receive exemption from remediation. See, for example, the story of David's sin and restoration in 2 Samuel 11 and 12. While God shows mercy to David by putting away his sin of murdering Uriah the Hittite and stealing away his wife (see 12:13), justice nonetheless demands that the firstborn son of Bathsheba (conceived adulterously) die (see vv. 12–14). And Jesus does not tell the woman who is about to be stoned and everyone circled around her that they need to forget about her sin and give her another chance. In all of these cases, sin is clearly remembered, named, and accounted for.

The well-known parable Jesus tells in Matthew 18:23–35, often referred to as the parable of the unforgiving servant, conveys painfully clearly that in the kingdom of God justice is not set aside in deference to mercy. The king shows mercy to the servant who owes him an absurd amount, forgiving him of his debt. But then the forgiven servant goes out and demands that another servant pay him back everything that is owed. Fellow servants witnessing what has happened report the unforgiving servant's actions to the king. The king, in turn, demands that the unforgiving servant go to jail until he repays every last cent.

Mercy is clearly evident in this parable. The king extends it to the unforgiving servant. Justice is also apparent, both in the reporting of the community to the king and in the king's subsequent actions. When the fellow servants see the unwillingness of the forgiven servant to forgive another, they register this as injustice. Interestingly, if the unforgiving servant had not been forgiven by the king, his demand that he be repaid by the one owing him less would have been considered perfectly just. Perhaps this is the case, at least in part, because the unforgiving servant would have needed the money apart from the king's forgiveness. Important to note, for the purposes of our discussion, is that the merciful actions of the king both frame what is considered "just" in the context of the community and set a stage on which behavior that would otherwise be deemed acceptable and is technically lawful (that is, demanding payment for what is due) is now incomprehensibly unjust, low, and—somewhat ironically—unforgivable. In other words, the mercy proffered by the king has upped the ante for justice, and the entire community seems to know it, which is why they report the unforgiving servant for not acting in kind toward the other.

With mercy in play, it seems, treating people justly doesn't matter *less*—it matters *more*. "From everyone to whom much has been given, much will be required," Luke reminds us (Luke 12:48). Because mercy has been extended to us, we are called to give our treatment of others everything we've got, and then to give more. We are called to think creatively about what justice looks like in the context of mercy. To claim God's promise of daily bread in the context of remembering the gracious forgiveness of God is to know that no benefit is received because we have earned it or because we have certain rights. Doing justice, in light of mercy, is not about honoring rights. Rather, it is about recognizing and treating all people as the children of God, regardless of what they deserve.

Of course, this is where matters get tricky and where we need to get a bit creative. How *are* we at the same time to love mercy *and* to do justice, particularly when loving mercy and doing justice seem to conflict with each another? If loving mercy could simply be set aside, we could imagine the doing of justice as a challenging, but quite straightforward, task founded in requirements, rewards, and penalties. If the doing of justice could be tabled in favor of loving mercy, we could work to repress our judgments of those persons and systems responsible for breadless-ness and abuse, reminding ourselves that all of us are in varying degrees complicit and that it would be simplest, therefore, to forgive each other and move on. Both of these approaches to the problem of relating justice and mercy have, of course, been taken. And both are terribly lacking in the imagination it takes to participate in the kingdom. Let me examine each of them in a little more detail.

Mercy without Justice?

When it is separated from a commitment to justice, mercy is blind to the ways it perpetuates dynamics of oppression. The love of mercy readily becomes, in this case, a thinly veiled cover for those who are the perpetrators of injustice to place the burden of responsibility on those who have been treated unjustly. It also becomes an excuse, used by those who have been victimized, not to stand up and speak out against their abuse. The cover used by the perpetrator and the excuse offered by the victim work in tandem. The perpetrators of injustice encourage those who have been treated unjustly to be merciful, and these oppressed ones comply rather than complaining. Repentance and changed behavior on the part of the oppressors, if evident at all, tend to be viewed as optional bonuses rather than as indispensable hallmarks of healthy, life-supporting community.

The dynamic of mercy being forced on those who have been abused at the expense of doing justice is so habitual that, in recent decades, oppressed persons of faith have joined hands in naming and challenging it. One place where this has occurred is in a statement called the *Kairos Document,* published in South Africa in 1985. In this document, those who have been oppressed by the system of apartheid resist the suggestion that they need simply to forgive those who have abused them and appreciate the reparations being offered and changes to the system being made. They argue that "no reconciliation is possible in South Africa *without justice"* and that, biblically speaking, mercy is to be extended only to those who are deeply repentant and willing not only to make changes but to be fundamentally changed. "No reconciliation, no forgiveness and no negotiations are possible *without repentance,"* the document insists.[27] The document persuasively critiques the white minority who have the most political power in South Africa, noting that their unwillingness to allow blacks to take a leading role in shaping a new societal structure is indicative of a problem to which justice, and not (yet) mercy, is the appropriate remedy.

The *Kairos Document* addresses systematic abuses of people, justified by a leveraging of theological concepts such as "forgiveness" and "mercy" so distorted and extreme that thoughtful Christian believers realize the need to set them aside, for a time, if their life-promoting purpose is ever to be redeemed. In my view, however, it would be problematic if the document's statement—that forgiveness and the exercise of mercy can only follow after repentance and justice are in evidence—were extrapolated from the specific context in which the statement was made and applied more generally. After all (as discussed in Chapter 2), isn't it the case that the reality of God's grace precedes our active participation in and eventual transformation by it? And shouldn't the priority of the grace on which we first and ultimately rely be somehow reflected in the nature of our relationships to one another? How is it even possible to come to repentance apart from the work of grace, apart from the exercise of mercy?

The downside of theological arguments that attempt to correct the problems that come with prioritizing mercy at the expense of justice is that they often err in the other direction—that is, they put forward understandings of justice that distance themselves, in reaction to an abusive leveraging of the requirement that we love mercy, from the love of mercy itself. Let me raise some of the problems that can result from this.

Justice without Mercy?

Absent the exercise of mercy, the doing of justice can become more about claiming rights than developing relationships, more about meeting obligations than serving one another in love.

Certainly the claiming of rights *can* contribute to the flourishing of relationships, and it is almost always the case that the denial or abdication of rights harms relationships. A short story that poignantly illustrates this point comes from Amy Tan's popular collection *The Joy Luck Club*. The story "Without Wood" tells an all-too-familiar tale about a wife named Rose, whose husband, Ted, is leaving her for another woman.[28] More precisely, Ted wants Rose to leave their relationship and their house, so that he can marry the new woman, who can then seamlessly move in as Rose's replacement. Because Rose has always been overly compliant, Ted expects her to sign the divorce papers without question and move out of their house as quickly as possible. Realizing how much she loves the house and its garden, however, Rose has a kind of conversion experience in which she makes the uncharacteristically firm and noncompliant decision not to sign the divorce papers until Ted agrees that she will keep the house. She invites Ted over and tells him her mind, and his posture toward her changes. He sees her, suddenly, as a force with whom he must contend, as a person with whom he must negotiate in the context of their relationship. While it is probably too late for the marriage to be saved, Rose and Ted can still be in an authentic relationship, however contentious or amiable that relationship might be.

While remaining sympathetic to the ways Rose has been mistreated, "Without Wood" effectively conveys that her indecision and diffuse submissiveness have contributed to the marriage's failure. In doing this, the story demonstrates how the claiming of one's own rights and the respecting of these rights by others are essential components in authentic relationship. While other factors come into play, a relationship in which some function as if they have all rights and others as if they have none can be characterized only as dysfunctional and codependent.

Scripture seems to talk a lot less about claiming one's own rights than about looking out for the interests of others. As those who love mercy, who are continuously undone and remade by the profound working of grace, we are called to die to ourselves rather than to be self-protective. Does talk of respecting rights, and even doing justice, in any way contradict this? I would argue that it does not necessarily, though it can sometimes. This is because there must be rights before they can be given up, there must be a self before it can be denied, and there must be a system of justice in relation to which merciful actions can be taken. Submission is simply an incoherent notion when that which is being given up has not even been acknowledged. Only when the rights of the parties involved are known and respected does Paul's exhortation that we submit "to one another out of reverence for Christ" (Ephesians 5:21) even makes sense. It is only when we know our rights that we can intentionally set them aside to be fully present to one another.

Once this is understood, it is possible to make the assertion we often jump to too quickly, and at the expense of human flourishing. The claim is: The setting aside of rights, and not the claiming of them, is the pivotal component of the best relationships. While one must have rights to set them aside, only in and through setting them aside does intimacy become possible.

These rights are still had even as they are voluntarily set to the side for the sake of communion. These rights never dissolve. They are not set to the side because someone is being blackmailed into taking such action—such as a wife being forced to do exactly what her husband says, because otherwise she would find herself out on the street; or a black person in South Africa saying he supports "separate but equal" legislation, because he fears that if he said what he thought he would be physically harmed. Rather, they are set to the side because the people doing so realize that laying claim to the promises of God entails extending to others the grace that has been offered to us. In other words, the love of mercy allows for technical claims of justice to be set aside precisely so that we can live justly, in the deepest sense of the term. Let me explain this in a little more detail.

When a merciful spirit is absent, the doing of justice relies, for its motivation, on the presupposition that everyone has rights. Everyone has a right to a fair trial; everyone has a right to food and shelter; no one should be controlled through the use of violence. We are still debating about whether everyone has the right to the same quality of health care.[29] The stronger the belief in rights, the stronger the impetus for justice. The weaker the case for rights, the weaker the case for justice.

But if, in the midst of the work for justice, mercy is present, a value more gripping than rights begins to permeate the system. This value is that people should be treated well not because they have rights, or treated less well only when they have somehow forfeited these rights, but because they are people created and embraced by a gracious, forgiving, life-giving God. Because we belong to this God "in life and in death"—for this reason alone!—our lives are precious and valuable. When we love mercy (viewing ourselves, and one another, as children of this merciful God), we do justice not out of obligation, nor even out of respect for the inalienable rights of others, but as an extension of our cognizance that all creatures are created by God to live, to love, and to flourish. With mercy in play, just judgments are never solely about payback or punishment. Rather, penalties consistent with justice founded in mercy always manifest a desire for wholeness, recommending retribution only insofar as it contributes to restoration.

It is easier to assent to this in theory than in some circumstances. In particular circumstances, it is hard to know what it means to love mercy or to act kindly to those who need forgiveness. When crimes are so violent and heinous that restoration is unimaginable, mercy might seem to be such an incoherent notion that all it seems just to do is lay mercy to the side and punish. Interestingly enough, however, we also have problems with implementing mercy in cases where restoration is not only imaginable, but also evident. A compelling example of this is how we responded to the case of Karla Faye Tucker, a woman convicted of murder in 1984 and executed in 1998 even though it was clear that her life and behavior had been transformed by her conversion to Christianity.[30] Tucker was the first woman to be executed in the state of Texas since 1863. Because I live and teach theology in Austin, Texas, I was especially engaged in conversation and debate about how we were called both to do justice and love mercy in relation to the case. One story from this time period illustrates how much easier it is to divorce mercy from justice rather than to imagine the ways God is calling us to hold them in tandem.

It was late in the spring semester of a class I teach titled "Theological Reflection in Contemporary Society." I forget exactly what subject I was lecturing on, but on the way to class I stopped by my mailbox and found I had been sent one of those "WWJD?" lapel pins. Remember those pins? This one was extra special: It had a little battery in it, and a little light. When you pressed the button to the side of the WWJD? it blinked.

On a whim, I pinned this thing to my jacket, turned on the blinking light, walked into class, and began to lecture. A few minutes into my lecture, one of my crasser students interrupted to ask why I was wearing that "&*@#!" blinking-light pin. "What—this?" I asked, feigning surprise at his question. "Why, this is a WWJD? pin. Do you have a problem with that?" I then launched into guiding a discussion that I imagined marvelously displayed my brilliant pedagogy. The bottom line of the conversation was this: Of the twenty-nine mainly Presbyterian, some Methodist, and a couple of "other" students who were there, every single one emphatically agreed that if and when we *do* know what Jesus would do we should certainly do it.

Having this gratifying statistic in hand, I turned the conversation to Karla Faye Tucker and the biggest news story in Texas that week. Tucker, a convicted murderer and rehabilitated born-again Christian, was due to be executed in a few days. There was unbelievable pressure on the governor to commute her sentence, since her conversion and rehabilitation seemed genuine.

We took a vote, and twenty-nine of the twenty-nine students present agreed that Jesus would *not* execute Karla Fay Tucker.

Then something strange happened. Before I could turn the conversation to a discussion of how we, as people of faith, should (or shouldn't) get involved in the politics of the debate, twenty-seven of the twenty-nine students in the class suddenly and emphatically reneged on their commitment to do what Jesus would do. Twenty-seven of the twenty-nine students insisted that we *should* execute Karla Faye Tucker, putting forward the argument that it would be "presumptuous" to think that we could ever do what Jesus would do. One of these students proposed that, in all humility, we replace our WWJD? buttons with a different set of letters: WWJWUTD? (What would Jesus want us to do?). Clearly, the student argued, Jesus would want *us* to execute Tucker, even if he wouldn't do it himself. Jesus is at liberty to forgive; we, with our sinful identities in place, can only do the next best thing.

My beloved students—future (and now current) ministers—set mercy aside when they couldn't figure out how to reconcile it with justice. And I, for my part, didn't do much better. Stunned and disappointed by the class's support of the WWJWUTD? argument, I was at such a loss at what to do next that I ended class early. I was discouraged. I had lost sight of the kingdom, and for this reason wasted an important opportunity to recall the class to a love of mercy, to bear passionate and prophetic witness to the power-full working of grace, to imagine the unimaginable.

A More Imaginative Integration

While I agree with the *Kairos Document*'s criticism of the Empire's distorted promotion of forgiveness as a means of preserving the power of those who have had authority, I am less certain about its implication that repentance can occur *first,* and then be met by a merciful response. Reformed theology has always held, along these lines, that repentance is precipitated *by* the working of grace; it is only when we realize we have been restored to the wholeness of our created identity that we can begin to acknowledge just how wretched we've become. As was mentioned in Chapter 2, it is only after we have sung "Amazing grace, how sweet the sound" that we are able to acknowledge the "wretch like me" that it has saved.

Acknowledging both that the *Kairos Document* is correct that there can be no mercy without justice and that the work of repentance and openness to transformation necessary for justice to take place might never happen apart from the movement of grace, it is time to think a little more creatively about this. My suggestion would be to imagine mercy and justice somehow occurring simultaneously, rather than in a particular order that requires one to be necessary for the other to be possible.

It would be useful to make the distinction between the ontological[31] reality of God's grace-full, merciful, unconditional claim on us and the epistemological[32] need for persons, and systems, to operate in ways that are fair and just. It seems to me that, in making this distinction, we can say that justice and mercy have priority at one and the same time. From an ontological standpoint, the unalterable reality is that we are loved, claimed, reconciled, forgiven, and righteous. In genuinely realizing this, we begin to enter into the process of being changed in the way we live. From an epistemological standpoint, what matters most is how we live and act in the world—all the talk of being "loved unconditionally," "forgiven for our sins," and "made righteous in Christ" is meaningless when we are not doing the right thing by the other. The movement is not simply *from* mercy *to* justice, and it is not that it is merely *from* acting justly (or being treated justly) *to* receiving mercy (or extending mercy). Rather, the arrows are, at one and the same time, moving both directions. Surely, this "double movement" is what Reformed and Lutheran theologians had in mind when they debated about the relationship between law and grace. Certainly, it came into play in Luther's articulation that we are at the same time righteous (recipients of mercy) and sinners (those who struggle to do justice). Finally, thinking imaginatively in terms of the simultaneity of mercy and justice leads readily to a reading of the parable of the unforgiving servant that recognizes neither mercy nor justice is prioritized over the other. Mercy is the starting point, ontologically (it is the reality in which the unforgiving servant leaves the king's presence, though he doesn't recognize it). And justice is the starting point, epistemologically (it just doesn't matter that mercy is the ontological reality, when he doesn't act in accordance with it). We need to begin, simultaneously, with both mercy and justice.

And when we do, we have glimpsed the kingdom of God, where there is perfect continuity between loving mercy and doing justice, between the ontological and the epistemological, between being and doing. In the kingdom there is perfect freedom. Augustine taught that the kingdom is the place where we, as Christian believers no longer bound by sin, are perfectly free to choose "only the good."[33] That is, as those living perpetually in full awareness of the grace of God, we also live as those who are bone sure of who we are: children of God who belong to God "in life and in death." And we act accordingly. We act not like that unforgiving servant (who acts inconsistently with who he is), but much like those clueless sheep in Matthew 25 (who act so consistently with who they are that they don't even realize they have acted).

While the communion of justice and mercy will be fully realized only in the *eschaton,* this does not mean we can wait to integrate the two until then. We may not cease worrying, in this world, about honoring the doing of justice and the love of mercy simultaneously, even if this means continuously shifting back and forth between the two as we engage them dialectically.

Note that this is a common phenomenon in Christian theology, precisely because we are striving to understand and live into those things that are beyond our comprehension, the things of God that are not limited to time and space. For example, we think of human beings as being at once righteous and sinners, but since it is tough to think simultaneously in both these categories we probably move back and forth between them. Similarly, we believe Jesus is both fully human and fully divine, and that the triune Godhead is both one in three and three in one. In other words, we habitually invite participation in dialectical tensions as a way of remembering the mysterious character of what we believe.

Living into and out of these dialectical tensions certainly keeps us humble. We will probably, at times, even throw up our hands in frustration at how impossible it is for us, who are limited by space and time, to honor truths that exist simultaneously. Not accidentally Micah 6:8 lists walking humbly with God as the third requirement—it follows *from* our efforts both to do justice and to love mercy, and to do both without compromising on either! To walk humbly with God is to remember always the limitations we have, as creatures in this world, in understanding these things. Even our best efforts for the sake of the kingdom are provisional ones. It is to affirm, as we say every time we pray the Lord's Prayer, that the kingdom promised to us, which is coming to earth as it is in heaven, is God's.

Walking Humbly with God

How can we imagine our lives characterized by a humble walking with God? And how can our humility possibly promote social righteousness, facilitating the coming of the kingdom to earth, as it is in heaven?

Humility is a tricky thing to imagine, since imagining it seems immediately to undercut it. In other words, picturing ourselves as humble, and then striving to *be* humble, seems to be a pride-full, not a humble, endeavor. On some level, our recognition of this dilemma is evident in the jokes we make about trying to be humble. "I've been working at being humble," we might say. "Pretty soon I'll be the humblest person I know!"

Micah 6:8 advocates not that we focus on our own humility, but on humbly walking *with God*. The focus is not first and foremost to be on who we are and how we can improve ourselves, but rather first on who God is and then on who we are in relationship to this God. Following the program delineated on the chart introduced early in this book, the argument of this final section of the chapter is that our humble walking with God, part and parcel of the shape of social righteousness, is founded in the love of God that serves as its basis. When we live in cognizance of the mystery of God's love, we walk humbly, knowing our unworthiness even as we recognize our irreplaceability and value. In fact, awareness of our value to God evokes awareness of our unworthiness. "How can God love a sinner such as I?" we ask.[34] "How can it be that I—a virgin who is, in and of myself, incapable of having a child—am called to bear God to the world?[35] Don't you realize that I stutter?[36] How can you ask me, Jesus, if *I* love *you?* I am not worthy of being asked this question; I cannot possibly be the "rock" on which your church is built. Don't you remember that I denied you three times?"[37]

Even when we remember that our humble walking is accomplished not by concentrating on our own powers of renunciation, but by remembering who we are in relationship to our loving God, imagining what it "looks like" to be humble can be tough for other reasons. The fact of the matter is that we associate humility with being "doormat-ish." We imagine the humble person as the faceless one, the serving one, the one who doesn't seem aware of his or her talents and would never think to worry about being self-fulfilled. And we, understandably, do not want to be this person.

Fortunately, in our better theological moments we know that something about these stereotypical images of what it looks like to be humble isn't quite right. Surely, we reason, whatever it means to walk humbly with our God, it can't contradict what it is to have a strong and centered identity as children who belong to God in life and in death, as those who are to stand "strong in the Lord and in the strength of the Lord's power" (Ephesians 6:10). But how do we reconcile spiritual strength with humble walking?

Spiritual strength and humble walking go hand in glove. When we stand strong in the *Lord* we walk humbly, since standing strong in *ourselves* puts ourselves, rather than God, in the center. Walking humbly with God, then, entails our constant repenting of the sin of pride. Consistent to some degree with stereotypical understandings, to walk humbly with God is, on the one hand, ever to be de-centered, when it comes to preserving our own importance and power. As Christ empties himself, taking the form of a servant, so we—in the context of our humble walking—are continuously emptied of any sense of entitlement so that we might serve one another freely.

On the other hand, to walk humbly with God is also to be continuously re-centered, when it comes to our own value and power. As Christ rose up to be the ruler of all, so we—as those who walk humbly with the God who exalts us in him—are raised to full participation in the life and work of God. Popular stereotypes to the contrary, then, walking humbly does not necessitate our becoming doormats. Rather, walking humbly with God is about *standing strong*. It is not about being lovingly hauled around (as a parent transports a toddler) but about perambulating, on our own two feet, as those who are Christ's friends (see John 15:15), as those who are his bride presented "without a spot or wrinkle . . . holy and without blemish" (Ephesians 5:27), as those who have been given "the ministry of reconciliation" (2 Corinthians 5:18). *How can this be?* Is it possible to imagine any stronger standing, or one that fills us with a deeper sense of humility?

Two questions that follow from such reflections are: (1) What does it look like, more precisely, to walk humbly with God? and (2) How do we imagine that our humble walking promotes social righteousness? In the remainder of this chapter, I will offer some initial responses to these two related questions.[38]

First, what challenges does walking humbly with God lay before us? Two biblical images that help me imagine the concrete shape and challenges of walking humbly are that of the Israelites collecting manna (see Numbers 11:1–9) and that of Christ entering fully into existence with us, even to the point of death (see Philippians 2:1–13).

Manna—Humble Pie—in the Wilderness

In the Numbers 11 text, the Israelites are getting so sick and tired of collecting, preparing, and eating manna every day that they begin reminiscing. "Oh, how we miss the fresh fish we used to eat in Egypt!" they complain. "Remember those crunchy cucumbers and juicy melons? And what I wouldn't give for some leeks, onions, and garlic!" God is, to put it mildly, not pleased with the people's complaints. God gets angry, it seems, not because the people yearn for a greater variety of things to eat but because the people have disparaged their own manna-gathering community in favor of their former lives in Egypt.[39]

To understand how imagining the Israelites collecting manna might help us grasp the challenges of walking humbly with God, it might be useful to review the "rules" surrounding manna.

One of the interesting things about manna is that every person is entitled to exactly the same amount per day. That's all that can be collected; anything extra will rot. If any family is harboring an illegal slave and tries to collect a portion of manna for that slave, their efforts will be in vain and their crime found out. So manna is a kind of great equalizer. One cannot get ahead of one's neighbors by working harder than them, or storing up for a rainy day, or developing more efficient harvesting techniques. In both the food and the size of its portion, the people share together. In its daily collection and preparation, the people join in the work of feeding, the work that sustains.

It seems to me that eating manna, and only manna, every single day would be quite challenging. Even more challenging than getting sick of eating manna would be, at least for me, *collecting* the manna every day, and collecting it only in the amount needed. If one could collect enough for a whole week, or if one could get someone else to collect it at least some of the time, eating it for every meal might be tolerable. The combination of having to collect and pound each and every single day *and* having only manna cakes to show for it would get me down. I'm afraid I would be right there with the Israelites, weeping and complaining.

As in the case of doing justice, walking humbly with God is easier to imagine when we associate it with humanitarian activities that are done optionally and only periodically, even if habitually. For example, many people reading this have likely "done justice" by serving in a soup kitchen, and perhaps even "walked humbly" by sitting down and eating meals with those we have served. The problem is that the manna example challenges us to imagine even beyond such worthy endeavors, not only to serve others and not only to eat with those whom we have served, but also to collect and prepare food with those with whom we share life. To walk humbly with God is not to have an edge over others and then, benevolently, to share out of our abundance. It is not to go out of our way to "do something" for them. It is, rather, to be completely disinterested in having any advantage and truly interested in being with and for others. It is to let go of the impulse to rescue, and to stand in solidarity.

Humility of Christ: All the Way Down

At this point, the extraordinary imagery of Philippians 2 may effectively be brought into play. In the person of Jesus Christ, the hymn proclaims, God empties God's self of all advantage. Jesus has the edge of all edges—equality with God!—but he sets it aside to be with and for us. Note that it isn't that Jesus puts on a humanity costume and heads down here for a while, attempting to teach us some important things about God and counterbalancing our sinfulness before heading back to the advantageous position of being "just God." Jesus' time on this earth is not a thirty-three-year experiment, a benevolent staffing of the soup kitchen, a commendable act of charity. It is not that Jesus joins with us to a point, going beyond what can reasonably be expected but pulling back when we begin mixing him up with the people he is serving, when we call him a criminal, or when we decide to crucify him. As one astute participant in an adult education class I once taught shouted out, spontaneously and with conviction, when I asked about the meaning of the cross: "It means God held nothing back from us!"

The humility manifested in Jesus Christ challenges any inclination we might have to think of the incarnation as a kind of "divine rescue operation" rather than an expression of love. One way some theologians imagine the significance of this is by playing with the popular narrative about the prince who disguises himself as a pauper to woo the beautiful maiden. Common versions of the story explain that the prince does this because he wants the maiden to love him for who he is, rather than for his wealth. In direct contrast to this, theologians have represented Jesus Christ as the prince who *doesn't* disguise himself as a pauper to woo us, but rather becomes the pauper to be with us and for us.[40] The pauper is who the prince is; the prince *is* the pauper. The fully divine one is fully human, and the fully human one is fully divine.[41] He gathers manna with us because he needs to eat. He shares with us the "umble" pie we have baked from scraps that are at hand. And he never flings aside his full humanity because it has served its purpose and is, therefore, over and done with.

Contrary to the typical narrative, the exaltation to which Philippians 2 bears witness does *not* represent the moment the prince shrugs off his humanity, revealing his true identity to the delight of the maiden who loved him even when she thought he was only a pauper. Rather, the maiden knows the *pauper*. It is the pauper she loves. If the pauper had been only a disguise, the maiden would have felt manipulated and disappointed. She who had loved the pauper would have been betrayed; she who had truly loved could only stand at a distance from the prince who was a stranger, from the stranger who had deceived her and broken her heart.

As a pauper, our prince who is Christ lifts us into the trembling-inducing reality of partnership, and power, and transformation. It is through being with and for us in our everyday, manna-collecting lives that he mystically becomes our manna. We eat his body, we drink his blood, our comings and goings and doings are grounded not in a particular agenda, but in his life as it extends outward, into the world. And change? Well, change happens from this place of abiding, and we are essential to it. "Therefore," writes Paul, "work out your own salvation with fear and trembling; for it is God who is at work in you, enabling you both to will and to work for God's good pleasure" (Philippians 2:12–13). *We* contribute something to what God is doing in the world, to the coming of the kingdom of God to earth, as it is in heaven. And we contribute something in and through—and only in and through—our humble walking with God, our working out of our salvation, our abiding in Christ.

Jesus Christ's obedience to God, even to the point of death on the cross, is our ultimate model for walking humbly with God. The point is not that we are called to die, but that we, like Christ, are called to hold nothing back from those whom we are with and for. No extra manna in our purses, no extra divinity hidden in the pocket of the Jesus of Nazareth costume, is permitted. And we can't get off the hook, on the humility requirement front, by claiming it is presumptuous to try to do what Jesus would do. We can't get off the hook, because Paul makes our instructions, this time around, perfectly clear: "Let the same mind be in you that was in Christ Jesus," he exhorts us (v. 5).

Needless to say, Paul sets the bar for us pretty high (or—should we say—pretty low!) when it comes to the humility standard. What would it look like for us to have the mind of Christ, as Paul describes it? Certainly, it must be that to walk humbly with the God who has entered fully and humbly into relationship with us is to enter fully and humbly into relationship with each other. And to enter fully and humbly into relationship with each other is, inevitably, to sacrifice some of what we might be able to do and to be if we didn't have to take the other into account. It is to put aside "being all we can be" in favor of submitting to whom—and what—that other person is. It is to kneel down with them and collect our allotted portion of manna, day after day, without looking over our shoulder at ways we might gain on them, benefit from them, or even rescue them. Such a requirement poses a serious challenge to us, who can imagine kneeling down only as visiting manna collectors, but not as those who need to come, every day, in order to eat.

Confident Humility

Having begun to discuss what it "looks like" to walk humbly with God, I will continue these reflections by responding to the second framing question posed, that is: How is it that our humble walking with God promotes social righteousness in such a way that it advances the coming of the kingdom?

To be perfectly frank, humility does not appear to be the best posture for world-changing, at least at first glance. From a distance, it is hard to construe the manna-collection scene as fostering anything other than passivity and doormat-ishness. What does gathering one's own sustenance, each and every day, side by side with others doing the same, have to do with the coming of the kingdom? It is no wonder our strategy, as go-getters who want to change the world for the better, is often to skip the manna and do whatever we can to develop a better menu. We are eager to find ways to import some fish, and cucumbers, and garlic; we are willing to go out of our way to help and to change.

Surely, anyone working through this book wants to do more than describe and/or reproduce the world. The point is, we believe, to change it. But here's the basic rub when it comes to humility: We are called to change the world not by focusing on change, but by abiding in Christ. When we focus on change, humility is displaced by what we perceive to be the more important work of "doing things" for people.

When we share in the mind of Christ, however, the things we do for others are merely an extension of our being for and with them. Like those good ol' dumb, humble sheep in Matthew 25, we don't even remember that we have fed, and clothed, and visited.

"Let the same mind be in you that was in Christ Jesus," Paul instructs (Philippians 2:5). Clearly, Jesus in his own mind never aimed to be a revolutionary, though his life clearly had a revolutionary impact. To have the mind of Christ, it seems, is neither to describe the world nor to change it, but simply to love it.

We promote social righteousness, then, not because we are aiming to incite a revolution, but because God has promised us a world where there is no more war, or pain, or sorrow. Because grace is of an altogether different order, we are able to expect the impossible things God has promised. And love compels us to live as though the kingdom God has promised *is* our place of residence, as those who know that *this* world—with all its pain and suffering—is not our home (see 2 Corinthians 5). And here's the twist: In love, we live at the same time both as those for whom this world is not our home *and* as those who deeply love the world that God so loves. "In the world, but not of it," Paul has said.

To live "in the world, but not of it" is a bizarre endeavor. It would make sense, I think, simply to hate the world, as those committed to promoting social righteousness. We could, readily enough, posture ourselves to live with moral outrage. Indignant about the corruption, the sin, the godlessness that surrounds us, we could forswear the world, refusing to concede our participation in it.

We could certainly claim plenty of biblical precedent for taking such a stance. Jesus, driving out the moneychangers. Paul, writing colorful lists of the sins of this world, insisting that Christian believers live their lives as those set apart. We are given specific instructions to reject conformity to this world (see Romans 12:2), to set our minds on "things that are above" (Colossians 3:2) rather than things on this earth, to "fight the good fight of the faith" in our pursuit of godliness (1 Timothy 6:12), and to deny our family members and ourselves to be disciples of Christ (see Luke 14:26).

But we are called to love; we are called to have the mind of Christ. We are called to live and to act in the world, willing and working for God's good purposes because we abide in the one who has emptied himself of all advantage and lifted us, his brothers and sisters, to perfect participation in the life and work of God. Because God, in Christ, is with and for us, we are freed to be with and for one another—

submitting to one another in all humility and holding one another up, without spot or blemish, as fellow members of Christ's body.

To love the world as God so loves it is (as that member of my Sunday school class so well put it) to hold nothing back. Since I have already used "prince," "pauper," and "maiden" language, I might as well continue to sin boldly and bring "knights" and "dragons" into play, by way of illustrating what I mean by this.

Knights and dragons are pretty big in our house, these days, with my son and daughter. Our family spends a lot of time playing with toy dragons, reading dragon books, and engaging in deep, analytical discussion about the difference between dinosaurs and dragons. (Dinosaurs are *real,* but *extinct;* dragons are *pretend,* but *not* extinct.) As we sit in our living room doing all this, my eye is occasionally drawn to a work of art Bill and I bought when I was pregnant with Alexander and wondering if I'd be able to handle all the self-emptying things I would be called upon to do as a new mother. The piece is by artist Brian Andreas. It features a picture of a knight along with the following statement: " 'Anyone can slay a dragon,' he told me, 'but try waking up every morning and loving the world all over again. That's what takes a real hero.' "[42] Waking up every morning and collecting that manna, or changing that diaper, or heading to work, to class, or to the store. And doing these things not because we are obliged to do them, but because we genuinely love this world, even as God loves it, every day anew. To love the world with such tenacity is, of course, a tall (maybe even an impossible) order. There are those of us who on many days have trouble simply fulfilling our obligations, never mind freely engaging them in love. But still Jesus stands in the background, waiting . . . hoping . . . asking us that question: "Do you love me?" (John 21:15). The feeding of the lambs and tending of the sheep that take place in the course of our humble walking are meant not to be a burden on us, but to be an extension of love.

Liberation theologians have encouraged us, along these lines, for quite some time. Try as we might to convince them, they just won't let us rich people think it's enough that we send our money, cucumbers, or whatever other extra resources we have in the direction of the poor. Rescue operations, they remind us, are of little long-term value to the poor and are utterly useless for redeeming the rich. What the poor want is for the rich to join with them, to partner with them, to learn from and be corrected by their spirituality. To empty themselves and enter into solidarity with the other. To learn to love the world, each and every morning, all over again.

Letty Russell makes an observation that I believe slices right into our ambivalent relationship with humility, highlighting our failure to love this world even as God loves it. In an unpublished public address, she said that the problem with the Presbyterian Church (U.S.A.) is that we are *of* the world, but not *in* it. She went on to annouce that she was giving up her ordination as a protest against what she identified as the "creeping clericalism" of the church. While we claim to uphold the "priesthood of all believers," Russell argued, we reinforce the hierarchies that perpetuate Empire.[43]

Of the world, but not *in* it. Could it be that we are missing out on enjoying the manna that is right under our shoes because our out-of-control appetites are driving us toward Egypt? In what ways are we buying into the creation of systems and agendas that keep us from being with and for one another even as God, in Christ, is with and for us?

We have the opportunity, right now and every day, to repent of our complicity in the destructive systems of the world. We should not repent because we hate the world, but because we desire to be more fully *in* it—to love the world the way God loves it. If we truly loved the way God loves, wouldn't we invite others to participate in God's boundless grace, brazenly claiming God's promises with the pure confidence of children?

May God grant us the grace to share together in the mind of Christ. To empty ourselves of privilege that stands in our way of being with and for one another. To look at one another as better than ourselves, and take others' interests into account. To will and to work for God's good purpose as those who insist on imagining what God is up to, astounded that we are fully included in Christ. May we come to know, ever more deeply, the joy of walking humbly with our God.

Study Questions

1. What does it mean to "do justice"? How is our doing of justice grounded in recognition of God's promise to us?

2. What does it mean to "love mercy"? How is our loving of mercy grounded in our full participation in the grace of God?

3. Are you convinced by the author's argument that mercy does not give us a way to escape justice, but rather deepens our commitment to it?

4. What does it mean to "walk humbly with God"? How is walking humbly related to our deepening perception of God's love for us?

Notes

1. See, for example, suggestions made at actsofkindness.org.
2. *Eschatology* means "words about the end." It is a theological term that references the church's teachings about the second coming of Christ, the resurrection of the dead, and the creation of a new heaven and a new earth. Contemporary theologians insist that eschatology concern itself not only with the future, but also with the relevance of our beliefs about the future to the here and now. Thus, the doctrine of eschatology is often identified as the "doctrine of Christian hope."
3. When I talk about imagining the kingdom of God, I am not advocating we imagine a world that is fun and inspiring but will never come to be. I am recommending that we imagine a kingdom that is both future and present, a world that is at the same time both the kingdom of God that is coming to be and the "real reality" that contrasts, even now, to this pain-full world that is not our home. See, for example, 1 Peter 2:11.
4. From Calvin's Sermon No. 10 on 1 Corinthians, as quoted by William J. Bouwsma in *John Calvin: A Sixteenth-Century Portrait* (New York: Oxford University Press, 1988), pp. 134–135.
5. From Calvin's Commentary on Psalm 104:31, as quoted by Bouwsma, p. 135.
6. *Institutes,* I.13.1.
7. *Institutes,* I.13.17, quoting Gregory of Nazianzus, *On Holy Baptism,* oration XL.41.
8. I imagine, rather, that Calvin's stack includes a Bible, a copy of Augustine's *Confessions,* and possibly the latest review of the imaginative theological statements developed at the great ecumenical councils (including the Chalcedonian statement of 451, which invites us into full participation in God precisely by way of its creative insistence that Jesus Christ is *both* "fully human and fully divine").
9. Guillaume Farel, who insisted he come to Geneva.
10. For this reason, a large monument to Calvin and other religious figures who upheld religious liberties is the centerpiece of the town park in Geneva. To see a picture of this monument, go to sacred-destinations.com/switzerland/geneva-reformation-monument.htm. For more on the complexities of Calvin's relationship to modern conceptions of religious freedom, see the Center for Public Justice's review of William Stevenson's *Sovereign Grace* at cpjustice.org/stories/storyReader$559.
11. It must be noted, at this point, that Calvin's support of the execution of Servetus was simply wrong. For a balanced discussion of this, including mention of Calvin's failed attempt to minimize Servetus's suffering, see Marilynne Robinson's "Marguerite de Navarre" in *The Death of Adam* (New York: Houghton Mifflin, 1998), pp. 174–206, especially pp. 200–206.
12. For more on what Calvin accomplished along these lines, see a site created by the Presbyterian Church (U.S.A.) on the occasion of the five-hundredth anniversary of Calvin's birth (1509): pcusa.org/calvinjubilee/society.htm.
13. *Institutes,* II.3.13.
14. While wormwood has been used throughout history for positive medical purposes, its bitter flavor is seemingly being evoked here. Justice, metaphorically speaking, is made "bitter" by those who disrespect it.

15. This idea is commonly identified, particularly in Roman Catholic moral theology (especially in the theologies of liberation theologians including Gustavo Gutiérrez), as the "preferential option of the poor."
16. *CD*, III/4, p. 544.
17. I first heard this turn of phrase from the late Letty Russell.
18. Barth's phrase. See *CD*, III/4, pp. 552–553.
19. *CD*, III/4, p. 552.
20. Barth's term.
21. For more on a theology of play, see my " 'Beautiful Playing': Moltmann, Barth, and the Work of the Christian," in *Theology As Conversation: The Significance of Dialogue in Historical and Contemporary Theology,* eds. Bruce L. McCormack and Kimlyn J. Bender (Grand Rapids: Wm. B. Eerdmans, 2009), pp. 101–116.
22. Deborah Miller, "Justices Deny DNA Testing as a Right to Prisoners," *Cleveland. com,* June 18, 2009, cleveland.com/nation/index.ssf/2009/06/justices_deny_dna_testing_as_a.html.
23. For an overview of Lehmann's contribution along these lines, see Nancy J. Duff's *Humanization and the Politics of God: The* Koinonia *Ethics of Paul Lehmann* (Grand Rapids: Eerdmans, 1992).
24. This is an allusion to John 15:15.
25. Daniel Hartnett, "Remembering the Poor: An Interview with Gustavo Gutiérrez," *America: The National Catholic Weekly,* February 3, 2003.
26. Notice that the Hebrew term *hesed,* in Micah 6:8, is usually translated as "kindness" or "mercy." Its meaning is impossible to capture in English, connoting both God's unconditional love for and loyalty to us. One well-known hymn that bears witness to the resonances of *hesed* is "There's a Wideness in God's Mercy." Written by Frederick William Faber, this hymn integrates reference to God's mercy, love, kindness, grace, compassion, and fondness for us. The full lyric can be found at scriptureandmusic.com/Music/Text_Files/Theres_A_Wideness_In_Gods_Mercy.html.
27. "Reconciliation," *Kairos Document* (Johannesburg, 1985), section 3.1, http://www.sahistory.org.za/pages/library-resources/official%20docs/kairos-document.htm.
28. Amy Tan, "Without Wood," *The Joy Luck Club* (New York: Penguin Books, 1989).
29. Further examination of this subject will take place in Chapter 4.
30. For a brief overview of Karla Faye Tucker's life, see en.wikipedia.org/wiki/Karla_Faye_Tucker.
31. *Ontological* has to do with "being," or what is.
32. *Epistemological* has to do with how we come to know or learn what is.
33. This well-known teaching of Augustine is, not surprisingly, a controversial one for those who disbelieve there can be freedom apart from the opportunity to choose against the good.
34. An example of a hymn that asks this question is Charles Gabriel's "I Stand Amazed in the Presence." The full lyrics to this hymn may be found at hymnsite.com/lyrics/umh371.sht.
35. An allusion to Mary's response to the angel Gabriel in Luke 1.
36. An allusion to Moses' response to God, speaking to him from the burning bush in Exodus 4.
37. An allusion to Peter's response to Christ in John 21.
38. Portions of the paragraphs following are taken from "Umble Pie," a sermon I preached at the 218th General Assembly of the Presbyterian Church (U.S.A.) in

San Jose, California, on June 26, 2008. This sermon is published in the summer 2008 edition of Austin Presbyterian Theological Seminary's *Windows,* which is available online at austinseminary.edu/uploaded/about_us/pdf/windows/windowsfall2008.pdf.

39. See, as evidence for this, verse 18. Notice that neither God nor Moses berates the people for being sick of manna, but for their former, enslaved lives in Egypt over their humble existence as the people of God.

40. This is a crucial theological point I learned from Kierkegaard (see *Philosophical Fragments,* especially Chapter 4) and Barth (see especially volume IV/2 of *CD*).

41. This sentence reflects the Christological statement adopted at the Council of Chalcedon in 451.

42. Reference to this quote may be found on many Web sites, including goodreads.com/quotes/search?q=%22anyone+can+slay+a+dragon%22&commit=find+quotes.

43. From an unpublished presentation Dr. Russell gave the spring of 1996, at a conference on justice held at the Plaza Resolana in Sante Fe, New Mexico.

4

Embodying the Kingdom: The *Fruit* of Social Righteousness

> Righteousness exalts a nation,
>   but sin condemns any people.
>   —Proverbs 14:34 (TNIV)

This final chapter offers several reflections on what the promotion of social righteousness might look like in relation to specific issues facing us in our current American context. These reflections are drawn from an online piece I write for a blog called "Texas Faith" that is part of the Religion section of the *Dallas Morning News.* Each week, several religious experts answer questions having to do with the relationship of our faith commitments to what is going on in our contemporary (usually political) context. The answers are posted every Tuesday, and are often excerpted in the Saturday print edition.[1]

Sharing several of my "Texas Faith" answers as a way of closing this book is a bit risky for at least two reasons. The first is the political one: Christians do not always agree on things, and I do not want to distract attention from the main themes of the book by opening up controversial political issues right here at the end. However, what good would a book on promoting social righteousness be if it avoided the concrete issues facing us merely for the sake of escaping conflict and ending smoothly? It seems to me that all our talk of promises, grace, and love; justice, mercy, and humility must pan out somehow in relation to those matters that concern us most. In the final analysis, theorizing about justice is pointless if bread is not distributed. Hoping for mercy, if one does not forgive, is hypocritical. And posturing humility, when one is vying for more power in this world, is profoundly deceptive.

What we believe about promoting social righteousness better have corporeal consequences—it better, in fact, promote social righteousness! We ponder the complexities of justice with the desire to move bread into someone's mouth; we struggle to think through the relationship between forgiveness and mercy and imagine facilitating reconciliation; we are filled with strong conviction about the deliverance that comes with walking humbly with God, determining that we will challenge the oppressive structures of the world.

Given these impetuses, a book on social righteousness must contain explicit reference to the issues of our day, even if we do not agree on how these issues should be addressed. So let me say, from the outset, how keenly aware I am that the views I regularly post in "Texas Faith" will not be met with universal agreement. My intention (for the purposes of this chapter) is not to provoke a debate with the reader on any of the particular issues. Rather, I offer these examples in the hope that they model a faithful claiming of the appropriate *bases* for promoting social righteousness (God's promises, God's grace, and God's love) and a faithful imagining of the *shape* of social righteousness (characterized by the doing of justice, the love of mercy, and the humble walking with God) as presented in this book.

I believe that holding one another to account in relation to these bases and this shape will help facilitate and ground debates about what the promotion of social righteousness looks like in particular instances. Therefore, I offer my own reflections for the readers' consideration, analysis, and critique. I would be interested to know, for example, what readers think about how what I have said (in chapters 2 and 3) about God's promises, God's grace, and God's love comes into play (and does not) in the ways I have addressed the "Texas Faith" questions (in this chapter). And I would be curious to see if readers can identify where a commitment to doing justice, loving mercy, and walking humbly with God is in evidence.

A second reason offering concrete examples of what it might look like to promote social righteousness is tricky is that what it might look like will certainly change, depending on the context, the needs in play, the resources available, and the people involved. The examples from "Texas Faith" offered in this chapter were all written between August 2008 and August 2009, at a time when we were worried about the economy and health care, at a time when we were—understandably—not able to do much more than be angry with Madoff, Suleman, and/or Rumsfeld. If someone pulls this book off the shelf in 2016, and tries to apply what I have said about Suleman to some yet-unnamed person who appears, at first glance, to be involved in similar antics, the answers I have offered will probably not resonate. Even more likely, the Madoff, Suleman, and Rumsfeld examples will make the book seem more dated than it would otherwise appear.

In some ways, the risk of becoming outdated is simply the nature of the "promotion of social righteousness" beast. That is, one cannot promote social righteousness without addressing particular issues. And particular issues hold interest only for a particular period of time. But my hope is that, even when these examples become dated, they will continue to illustrate both the contextual nature of the enterprise and the enduring value of reflecting on the bases for and shape of social righteousness in whatever circumstances we are called upon to promote it.

In addition to these two concerns, one other point must be developed before reflecting on my "Texas Faith" answers. Simply put, to recognize that the church promotes social righteousness with the hope of seeing God's kingdom become manifest on earth as it is in heaven is at once also to acknowledge our significant limitations. Any contribution we make to the creation of the "fruit" of social righteousness is a provisional one. Any bread we are able to provide, any reconciliation we are able to facilitate, and any deliverance from evil we are able to encourage or inspire, while essential to the work of God in the world, is subject to critique and improvement. It is always only partial, when seen from the vantage point of the fullness of the kingdom.

Reference to the world to come and the eschatological claims related to it remind us of the provisional character of even our best efforts. The coming of the kingdom, for example, is closely associated with the second coming of Christ. And to believe in any sense that Christ is coming back again implies that there is a way in which he who is with us always (see Matthew 28:20) is also not presently here, at least not in all his fullness. We wait for Christ; we await the kingdom; we realize our work will never be complete apart from that final consummation, which is also the perfection of our redemption.

This provisional character of even our best work is not due solely to the practical reality that times and circumstances change. It is also related to the dynamic character of God's living and active Word. There is a sense in which everything said in this book about what we have to contribute to the coming of God's kingdom to earth, as it is in heaven, comes down to this: We are called, as the disciples of Christ, to be engaged in the process of discerning what God is up to in the world and going "there" to help out. While God's Word never changes, it is unchanging in its capacity to meet us ever anew, throwing us and all our would-be agendas into "crisis,"[2] and leading us to promote social righteousness in ways we might otherwise never have expected.

Because God's Word is impossible to pin down once and for all, some theologians avoid identifying it with certain perspectives on particular political matters. The concern is that, if such identifications are made, opinions about "what God wills" in a given situation will tend to be generalized and come to function idolatrously. Barth is concerned about this. When people of faith ask him to tell them what it is, specifically, that God wants them to do, Barth merely instructs them to obey the command of God. Barth is not averse to offering his opinion. He simply wants it to be understood that his opinion on a given issue—even an opinion he strongly believes is right—is always a provisional and contextual one.

Historically, as it turned out, Barth's fear that one of his contextual statements would be inappropriately universalized was realized. He issued "Nein!"[3] in relation to the natural theology he believed was being used by the German Christians to justify their support of Hitler. It was inappropriately applied, fifteen years later, to the communist East. Barth, understandably, was furious. "Everybody is rushing about today crying that the same 'No' must be said again . . . ," he complained. "As if such simple repetitions ever occurred in history! And as if the church were an automatic machine producing the same goods today as yesterday."[4]

That "simple repetitions" do not occur in history, coupled with the reality that submission to the living and active Word of God throws our agendas into question, reminds us of what we considered previously. That is, we are called to walk humbly with our God, faithfully living in and loving the world even as we are reoriented by the coming of the kingdom. The following answers, at best, are steps along the way, at once both provisional and essential to the divine work.

Bread

"Give us this day our daily bread," we pray. We have asked for the kingdom to come. We have recommitted ourselves to doing the will of God that will facilitate its coming. And now we are requesting that which is most needed, and most basic: the sustenance to live for another day.

The promise of God is that no one is forgotten. Every hair on every head is numbered. God loves all of us all the time, despite indications that seem to argue to the contrary.

When we ask for daily bread, we lay claim to the promise of God's care for, and provision for, "us." It is important to note that the prayer is not in the singular, but in the plural. Jesus taught us to pray to "our" Father for "our" daily bread. Given the character of God's promises, it makes sense to hope that all people are included in the "our." When we pray the Lord's Prayer, we should imagine all people receiving the daily bread they need to sustain them.

But what is included in the "daily bread" we request for all people, the bread for all people we believe is indicative of the kingdom of God? And what work are we called to do, in this moment, to facilitate all receiving this bread? Clearly, daily bread is meant to reference bread, tortillas, rice, potatoes, and other sustenance. There is no more important example of doing justice than getting food into the mouths of the hungry. But reference to daily bread also precipitates reflection on how we can work to make provision for other basic human needs, such as the need for shelter.

In our context, one of the matters right before our eyes is whether health care should be considered a basic right of all, a form of daily bread. At the time of this writing, we have little agreement on this matter, culturally speaking. Recently, I was asked to answer a question on this subject. The question and the answer appear below.

Question for "Texas Faith" Panelists (July 24, 2009)

The debate over health care has revolved, perhaps appropriately, around cost, availability, and the limits of partisan compromise. But is health care more than a political issue? Is it fundamentally a moral issue? And if so, doesn't that mean that providing expanded—or universal—health care is a moral imperative, not just a programmatic choice?

Catholic social teaching says that just societies are those in which basic needs are met. For those who believe that health care is a moral issue, the question isn't whether it should be provided: a just society must provide it. For those who see health care as a policy issue, the status quo and any of the variations under consideration in Congress are equally appropriate solutions, depending on our resources and our politics.

Here's the question: Is health care a moral issue? If so, doesn't that mean we must do whatever is necessary so that everybody has health care?

My Response

Providing health care for all must remain a programmatic issue precisely because it is a moral imperative. My observation is that policy makers by and large acknowledge the moral concerns related to health care. Even those who are against developing a universal health plan resist making the argument that the health of some is valuable while the health of others is expendable. In fact, they often make the (albeit debatable) point that "we already have universal health care" insofar as those who do not have health-care policies may nonetheless not be denied basic health care, which is covered by Medicaid. They frequently issue warnings that moving toward a socialized system of medicine would not result in all persons being adequately cared for but rather in many persons, currently being cared for, being neglected. While at worst these naysayers tend to be relatively wealthy, privileged folk who do not want to risk sacrificing anything related to their own care for the sake of making provision for others, they at best make the reasonable point that we simply cannot "do whatever is necessary" to provide health care for all. We cannot do whatever is necessary, they point out, because what it would be necessary to do is beyond our means.

I am someone who believes all should have full access to health care, and yet I share the fears of those who are opposed to developing programs that would provide it. I do not want to receive anything less, in terms of my health care and the care of my husband and children, than the very best my privilege allows us to receive. I want everyone to have the medical benefits we do, but at no cost to my family.

Early in my teaching career I visited a student of mine who had metastasized breast cancer. Nancy was in her early 20s and did not have health-care coverage. When the cancer recurred, she was denied treatment until a person with more privilege advocated for her. When I went to the hospital to see Nancy, I was brought to a wing I had never seen before in all my pastoral visits to the hospital. Instead of entering a private room, I was ushered into a large room crammed with patients and filled with a clattering din that made it difficult to talk or to pray together. Instead of beds, there were cots. While the food was served from a common cafeteria, there were no liners on the trays, as there were in the upscale wards. Too-few nurses appeared to be scrambling to keep up with the basic needs of everyone there.

Nancy died in that room.

When I think of Nancy, I am not suddenly more optimistic about making universal health care a reality. But I do recommit myself to considering how the impossible can be made possible, and what my role (and sacrifice) might be in facilitating this. Health care for all— and not only that "basic" health care that failed to provide Nancy with what she needed. Nancy should have had the best care we have to offer. God desires that all be fed to fullness, with twelve basketfuls left over, even if all we think we've got in hand is one boxed lunch. The promise we claim is that God makes the impossible possible. And so I can only pray, as a person of faith who pays attention to what it says in the newspaper: "Lord—help me now my unbelief!"

As people of faith we must actively refuse to settle into our disbelief, recommitting ourselves to doing whatever is necessary to realize God's kingdom on earth, as it is in heaven.

My Reflection

My answer incorporates several of the themes considered in this book. First, it attempts to appeal to the intrinsic worth of persons, rather than to rights and/or their respective levels of deservingness or undeservingness, as the basis for seeking to make universal health care possible. The doing of justice, as it is portrayed in the answer, resists buying into a zero-sum understanding of resources that focuses on fair distribution. It instead holds, as its backdrop, the image of Abram looking up at all those stars and believing that God will make possible what is otherwise impossible. The answer reflects, I think, a kind of straightforward foolishness about how this is all going to work, coupled with an honest confession of an unwillingness to sacrifice anything that I have, in terms of health care, for the sake of others. In this confession can be seen my struggle to have the mind of the Christ who emptied himself for my sake and the sake of the world—a testimony to how difficult it is to live, incarnationally, in true solidarity with the poor.

Forgiveness

"And forgive us our debts, as we forgive our debtors."

The next request we make in the prayer, and one that is presumably in continuity with the kingdom we have demanded, is forgiveness. Again, it is *our* debts, and *our* debtors, that stand in need of forgiveness and who pledge to forgive others. On a corporate level, forgiveness might be understood as the reconciliation of all—first to God, and then to one another. Grounded in grace, forgiveness is not something that is granted to us in exchange for repentance or in exchange for our forgiveness of others. Rather, forgiveness is something we are invited to participate in, as those who are saved by grace alone. It is when we are participating in it that we are brought to repentance, recognizing our wretchedness in relation to God's amazing grace. It is as we are participating in it that we ourselves come to love mercy, showing mercy to others almost as a natural extension of who we are—forgiven ones—in Christ. Insofar as we participate in the grace that supports our forgiveness, we see the other not as one who owes us or the one whom we owe, but as the one who is our brother or sister, the one with whom we share all things.

The problem comes, in the prayer and in life, when a person in the community is unaware that he or she is saved by grace alone. A person who is stuck in this way cannot be truly reconciled to the other, if reconciliation is about perfect participation in the life of God and in the lives of one another. This is because a person stuck in this way cannot imagine a life based in grace, but rather only a life founded in systems of exchange. These relationships, at best, can be ordered only in terms of what is owed and what is not owed; to establish relationships under such terms is to forego authentic communion.

One week I was given the tough assignment of thinking about all this in relation to the Bernie Madoff scandal.

Question for "Texas Faith" Panelists (March 17, 2009)

What does justice look like for Bernard Madoff? What do your faith systems suggest should happen to him? And what should he do, now that he's admitted guilt to what appears to be the largest financial swindle in human history?

My Response

Elie Wiesel, one of the most honest and thoughtful theologians I know, says justice for Madoff should look like this: "I would like him to be in a solitary cell with only a screen, and on that screen for at least five years of his life, every day and every night, there should be pictures of his victims, one after the other after the other, all the time a voice saying, 'Look what you have done to this old lady, look what you have done to that child, look what you have done,' nothing else."[5]

Wiesel is being criticized, because of this and other statements made about Madoff, for not exercising forgiveness. His response to such criticisms is that "forgiveness must be sought. . . and Madoff doesn't appear capable."[6]

I agree with both of Wiesel's comments I have cited because I understand the first in the context of the second. In other words,

Wiesel's recommendation that pictures of the victims be shown steadily for five years is a recommendation made for a person who is, as far as we can ascertain, incapable of seeking forgiveness. Wiesel believes Madoff's best hope for eventual humanization is to have the victims of his crime put continuously before him, every day and every night, so he will come to understand that what he did he did to people. (Interestingly, a similar strategy is employed in Holocaust museums, where visitors are exposed to continuous, videotaped testimonies of those who remember. We are shown the victims' faces; we come up against a pile of their shoes. We cannot escape their humanity, and so are driven to seek forgiveness.)

In my experience as a theology teacher, people of faith too often understand forgiveness as something that can be accomplished by the forgiver alone, apart from the participation of the one being forgiven. Not so. From the vantage point of the Christian tradition, Jesus consistently taught forgiveness isn't complete until the one being forgiven participates in its reality. In one of Jesus' parables on the subject, a king forgives a servant an impossibly large debt. Soon thereafter, that same servant forcefully demands that another servant pay him back a much smaller debt. Disturbed by this behavior, the unforgiving servant's peers report him to the king. The king immediately throws the servant in jail until he can pay "every last penny." The point of this parable is not that forgiveness is given, and then taken back. The point is that, until forgiveness is appropriated, the one who has been forgiven is not forgiven. So Wiesel is right to turn the accusation about his capacity to forgive Madoff to Madoff's capacity to pursue forgiveness.

Wiesel cannot imagine, and neither can I, that Madoff will be prepared to know forgiveness. But we, as people of faith, are called to pray anyway, even for impossible transformations we don't believe will take place. And—meanwhile—we need to show and see the pictures of those victims. Night and day, their faces need to be before us, that we might feel their pain, seek forgiveness, and insist on something altogether different.

My Reflection

My answer tries to take seriously the almost maddening contingency between *being forgiven* and *forgiving others*. This contingency is evident both in the prayer and in the parable of the unforgiving servant (which Jesus tells his disciples, following his instruction on the prayer, almost to underscore that there will be no compromise). Understanding the forgiveness of others less in terms of giving them something, and more in terms of standing in solidarity with them as fellow participants in grace, one can very carefully say that Madoff is not living in forgiving relationship with others, and therefore cannot be forgiven. He has not stood with others, he does not even seem to see them; his only hope for reconciliation is to be confronted with the faces of those others in the hope that seeing them will awaken him to cognizance of their shared participation, as fellow human beings.

My answer to the question clearly tries to apply to the Madoff case what I have written about the significance of *participation* to the promotion of social righteousness. When the faces of the other are not even seen (never mind respected or loved) it is social *un*righteousness that is promoted.

Also operative, in the background of my answer, is the idea that mercy, without justice, cannot effect genuine reconciliation. As the *Kairos Document* puts it, there can be no reconciliation without justice,[7] since only when people are treating one another justly can they live face to face with each other and share in the abundance of life. Mercy, apart from justice, excuses the perpetrator from acknowledging those who have been treated unjustly and therefore is an impediment to genuine reconciliation. Yet it seems a case is always being made for it. It is usually the victims who are told they must forgive and the perpetrators who are the nonparticipating "recipients" of forgiveness.

An example of this distortion can be seen in an ordination exam question, issued by the PC(USA) in September 1998. The students were asked to write a theological essay on "forgiveness" in response to the following, and specifically to address "Charlene's" concerns. The description of the case follows:

> Charlene, a member of the congregation which you serve as pastor, has made an appointment to talk with you. She says:
>
> My husband Roy has a temper. You and I both know what a good-hearted person he is. However, when he gets angry he seems to lose control, and sometimes he even hits me. He always shows remorse and says that he will not do it again, but the bruises don't go away. I have suggested counseling, but he says that he can handle it on his own.
>
> I try to forgive, but the memories are too painful. I feel guilty and confused because Jesus said we are supposed to forgive "seventy times seven." What does forgiveness mean in my situation?

"Charlene" seems convinced that forgiveness is up to her. She, like most of us, is thinking of forgiveness in terms of an exchange. Her husband "owes" her something, and it is her Christian responsibility to "forget" the debt. On top of suffering the abuse caused by her husband, she suffers guilt for not being able to do what she believes she should, as a Christian woman, be able to do.

Wiesel, in contrast to "Charlene," wisely refuses to be baited by the common but faulty theology that puts the onus of forgiveness on the victim. He understands what so many people of faith do not; that is, it is not for him to forgive Madoff, but for Madoff to recognize the grace-full character of existence and to enter into the dynamic of forgiveness himself. To enter into the dynamic is, by definition, not to forget, but precisely to remember. It is to remember and see, to repent and make right. Consider Zacchaeus, who, after entering into full participation with Jesus and his party guests, vows to pay back four times more than what he owes (see Luke 19:1–10). Or Scrooge, who wakes up after that redemptive night and cheerfully throws golden coins out to the people. He gives that money to those whom he had cheated without a second thought. Justice is done out of the love of mercy that is finally the reality. Forgiveness as reveling in the grace of God breeds forgiveness as solidarity with the other. Reconciliation, in turn, becomes the defining reality.

Deliverance

"And lead us not into temptation, but deliver us from evil."

The love of God compels a humble walking that turns its back on idols. Deliverance is turning away from what is not and turning toward what is. It entails emptying ourselves, over and over again, to God and one another. It is about loving this world as God loves it, about truly being with and for. To be delivered from evil is to be *free* to be who we are and never other than who we are. We are not little gods. We are not worshippers of idols. We are the children of the God who has created us, the God who has called us.

When we humbly walk with the God who loves us, we experience deliverance from all that is not real, true, and good. When we are reveling in the fact that the One who holds all the waters of the cosmos in the hollow of the divine hand is also the one who calls each of us by name, we remember our creatureliness and are not inclined to sin. We are, in fact, perfectly free, cognizant of who we are and acting accordingly.

Perhaps it can be fairly noted that walking humbly with God and its corresponding deliverance from evil, as characteristics of the kingdom of God, are those things that make all other forms of righteousness possible. Over and over again, it is turning away from participation in God toward that which is a distortion of God's creative and redemptive intentions that leads some to withhold bread from others, and many to settle for transactional, contractual relationships rather than to hope for participatory, covenantal ones. It is succumbing to evil that has ruined us. It is the damage wrought by our succumbing that necessitates our active promotion of righteousness.

Deliverance from evil is needed by everyone, from Rumsfeld to Suleman. With this in mind, I present two "Texas Faith" entries for this final section:

Question for "Texas Faith" Panelists (May 27, 2009)

The Pentagon's top-secret wartime memos that mixed Scripture and battle photos sparked a lively debate this week.

Over a photo of a U.S. tank entering Baghdad was a verse from Isaiah, "Open the gates that the righteous nation may enter, the nation that keeps the faith." Above another photo of a tank roaring through the desert was a quote from Ephesians, "Therefore put on the full armor of God . . . ." Some in the Bush administration worried that if the cover sheets got out, they could cast the Iraq invasion as a holy Christian crusade. Others saw no problem.

Religion is about absolutes; public policy is about subjective judgments. And yet, our currency invokes our trust in God, our leaders pray for divine guidance, and, apparently, the Pentagon annotates briefing memos with Bible verses.

So here's the question: When, if ever in our secular democracy, is it appropriate to advance public policy with God's words? When it is OK? And more the point, when does it cross the line?

My Response

Google immediately set before my eyes twelve of the cover sheets the question references. I am absolutely horrified, and more than a little surprised. I am surprised by how consistently and intentionally Scripture verses were used to affirm the "rightness" of the United States. Again and again, the assurance is made that "God is on our side" and that "therefore we must be in the right." While the first of these statements might very well be true ("In God we trust"—I do hope), it is not the case that the second necessarily follows.

I am horrified by these cover sheets not because "God's words" were used to "advance public policy," as the question asks. It is not as though we can carry God's words around with us in any book (even the Bible) and type them out on any piece of paper, over any picture we please. God exercises more jurisdiction than that over whatever it is God is meaning to say.

I am horrified, rather, because certain passages from Scripture were pulled completely out of context and overlaid on photos depicting our engagement in Iraq with no interpretative "bridge" in sight. By what hermeneutic (interpretive method), I wonder, did Rumsfeld and his staff place, atop a picture of a tank crossing the desert under a setting sun, Ephesians 6:13: "Put on the full armor of God . . ."? But verse 12 (directly preceding it), states explicitly that "our struggle is not against enemies of blood and flesh," and verses 14–17 (directly after it) make it clear that the "armor" is a metaphor for living lives marked by spiritual strength: truthfully, righteously, peacefully, and faithfully.

The words on those memos, I would argue, are not "God's words" even though they are, technically and literally, citations from the Bible. They are not "God's words," because the Word of God always speaks to, and from, a specific context in a specific way. My faith tradition (Christian and Reformed) understands the Holy Spirit to speak through the biblical witness as the Bible is interpreted by the Christian community. This interpretive work is hard work, requiring discipline and struggle, particularly when we are looking for blessing in circumstances that call for discipline and struggle.

In sum, we cross the line when we use God's Word to promote our own rightness or righteousness, and we cross the line when we forget that the Word of God became flesh—that it enters into specific contexts, and messes with what we think we understand about God, about ourselves, and about being right.

My Reflection

In my response to the Rumsfeld passage, I try to recall us all to a humble walking with God by reflecting on the purpose of the biblical text. Clearly, even the Bible can be used idolatrously—to promote human agendas, to distort perceptions of the will of God to establish "rightness." I also raise the concern, mentioned in this chapter, that the biblical text be read in context. Instead of gleaning from the text the verses that support our agendas, we should go to the text humbly, willing to empty ourselves to what God has to say about how we are to participate in *God's* agenda.

Rumsfeld is not the only one, in my view, who needs deliverance from evil. Consider my response to a question about the Suleman octuplets.

Question for "Texas Faith" Panelists (February 17, 2009)

The case of the Suleman octuplets has many angles. Initially there was amazement at the sheer medical feat of delivery. Then, as details about the mother filtered out, public attitudes turned from positive to, well, mixed at best.

Some critics focused on details about the mother—unmarried and unemployed. But others focused on the fact that she already had six children at home. This should, they suggested, have been more than enough.

But some religious traditions say there's no such thing as too many kids. Some Catholics and Orthodox Jews, for instance, have families as large as or larger than the Suleman family. So here's this week's simple question:

What does your faith tradition say about the Suleman case? Did she do anything wrong? Did her doctors? Or is this an example of science being properly used in the cause of new life, as desired by a woman who sees bringing new children into the world as her highest good?

My Response

Protestant Christianity does not, by and large, prohibit either birth control or the use of reproductive technologies. It does, however, exhort us to avoid idolatry.

Idols are the things we put between ourselves and God. To commit idolatry is to worship that which is of our own making rather than the one true God.

To engage in excessive behaviors that are ostensibly directed at promoting life can be a form of idolatry. Instead of accepting the limitations of our lives lived as creatures before the Creator God, we do whatever it takes to overwhelm them—to in fact become our own gods. This is, admittedly, tricky business. Where is the line between faithfully utilizing the God-given means that are at our disposal to foster life, and forcing ourselves into lives, and lifestyle patterns, that are idolatrous?

The line is easy to name, but harder to apply, given the complexities of life. But here it is: that which promotes the lives of us limited and wonderful creatures is on one side, and that which diminishes human and creaturely life is on the other.

And here is where it gets tricky, in the Suleman case, since Suleman and her doctors are ostensibly in the business of promoting life. If we could penetrate to the source of the rage that is being misdirected into violent threats against Suleman, we might well discover that it is, at root, a condemnation of behaviors that sap life, in the name of giving life, in a time in our history when many are struggling with how to promote life with increasingly limited resources at their disposal.

At the core of this rage, at best, is a recognition and resistance to idolatrous behaviors that insist on overriding creaturely limitations, building towers as high up in the sky as can possibly be built, oblivious to the fact that those who are standing on the ground are paying the bills.

But wait, I seem, in the preceding sentence, to have moved to another topic. Perhaps this food-stamp mom is merely mimicking the idolatrous behavior she has learned from her economic superiors, just in her own way.

My Reflection

In the above entry, I implicitly critique Suleman for not walking humbly with God. Like Rumsfeld, she makes an idol out of something unexpected. He makes an idol out of the Bible; she makes one out of childbearing. Not having the financial resources to "supersize" her life in the way the financial lords can, she figures out how to do it another way—reproductively. Turned away from the reality of her creaturely limitations and the promise of abundant life in relationship to God, she has forgotten to love this world in favor of trying to conquer it.

Study Questions

1. Discuss the author's take on the *Dallas Morning News* universal health care question. How does her answer reflect (and/or not reflect) the understanding of *justice* put forward in this book?

2. Discuss the author's answer to the question about Bernard Madoff. How is her understanding of *forgiveness,* developed in conversation with Elie Wiesel, consistent with what she has said about *grace* and *mercy?*

3. Compare the author's answers to the question about the Pentagon and the question about Nadya Suleman. What do these answers have to do with "deliverance from evil"? What is the relationship between *deliverance* and *humility?*

4. In what concrete ways can we embody the kingdom by doing justice, loving mercy, and walking humbly with our God?

Notes

1. To view these columns electronically, go to religionblog.dallasnews.com/archives/texas-faith.

2. This is an allusion to the "crisis theology" developed by Karl Barth, Emil Brunner, and other neoorthodox theologians.

3. "Nein!" ("No!") was an article Barth published in 1934 in response to a piece written by his colleague Emil Brunner. While Brunner was completely shocked by Barth's response, Barth believed Brunner had conceded too much when it came to theological methodology. Even trace amounts of natural theology, Barth held, had to be rejected.

4. Barth, "The Church Between East and West," *Karl Barth: Theologian of Freedom*, ed. Clifford Green (Minneapolis: Fortress Press, 1991), pp. 301–321.

5. Stephanie Strom, "Elie Wiesel Levels Scorn at Madoff," *New York Times*, February 26, 2009, nytimes.com/2009/02/27/business/27madoff.html.

6. Megan Barnett, "Wiesel Forgive Madoff? No," *Portfolio.com*, February 26, 2009, portfolio.com/views/blogs/daily-brief/2009/02/26/wiesel-forgive-madoff-no.

7. *Kairos Document*, 3.1.

Conclusion

One of the funniest bumper stickers I have ever read said this: "Look busy! Jesus is coming back!" While the message was clearly meant to mock those who put Rapture "warning" bumper stickers on their cars, it struck me as an inadvertent exhortation to me, a person of faith. I watch and I wait for the coming of my Lord. And when my eye is on the reality of the kingdom not of this world, I "get busy" in this one. My imagining gives way to service; my hope is realized in works of love.

What I want to reiterate, here at the close of this book, is simply this: The work of bringing the kingdom of God to earth, as it is in heaven, and the promotion of social righteousness that is integral to its coming, is all God's work. But it is also ours. It is ours because, in the person of Jesus Christ who has exalted us to full participation by the power of the Holy Spirit who makes Christ's presence known, God has claimed us as God's children, God's friends, and—even—as God's partners.

If there is one thing that I hope readers take away from this discussion, it is an understanding that we make a difference to the work of God in this world without jeopardizing one iota the reality of God's sovereign rule. We are essential contributors to this divine work because the sovereign God has promised that we are fully included; because this God is not a God who leverages sheer power, but a God of grace; and because we know the love of Christ that surpasses knowledge. Watching and waiting for the appearance of Jesus Christ, we engage in good works that are themselves a reflection of "heaven on earth," a witness to the promise of the kingdom. And through these efforts truly we serve as "salt" and "light" in this world, offering bread, forgiveness, and deliverance to those around us.

Along these lines, the prophet Isaiah showcases how our promotion of social righteousness makes a difference to those around us when he exclaims, "How beautiful upon the mountains are the feet of the messenger who announces peace, who brings good news, who announces salvation, who says to Zion, 'Your God reigns' " (Isaiah 52:7). We are called to be such messengers—messengers who do the justice that brings peace, love the mercy that is part and parcel of our salvation, and walk humbly with the God who reigns.

What we do in this world matters. It matters to the world today, and it matters to the world to come. It matters not because we have, in and of ourselves, the capacity to make the world a better place. It matters, rather, because *we* matter to the sovereign God who lives in solidarity with us, the God who desires that we be with and for each other, the God who yearns for us to share in God's love for this world that God so loves.

God created us, redeemed us, and is sanctifying us for perfect participation in the will of God, and full inclusion in the work of God. In fear and trembling, then—with the conviction that God is at work in us, enabling us to will and to work for God's good purpose—it is time to get busy, for Jesus is coming back. Thy kingdom come! Thy will be done! On earth, as it is in heaven.

Let us watch, and wait, and make it so.

Appendix A

Federal Council of Churches

(Now, National Council of Churches of Christ in the U.S.A.)

We deem it the duty of all Christian people to concern themselves directly with certain practical industrial problems. To us it seems that the Churches must stand—

For equal rights and complete justice for all men in all stations of life.

For the right of all men to the opportunity for self-maintenance, a right ever to be wisely and strongly safe-guarded against encroachments of every kind.

For the right of workers to some protection against the hardships often resulting from the swift crisis of industrial change.

For the principle of conciliation and arbitration in industrial dissensions.

For the protection of the worker from dangerous machinery, occupational disease, injuries and mortality.

For the abolition of child labor.

For such regulation of the conditions of toil for women as shall safeguard the physical and moral health of the community.

For the suppression of the "sweating system."

For the gradual and reasonable reduction of the hours of labor to the lowest practical point, and for that degree of leisure for all which is a condition of the highest human life.

For a release from employment one day in seven.

For a living wage as a minimum in every industry, and for the highest wage that each industry can afford.

For the most equitable division of the products of industry that can ultimately be devised.

For suitable provision for the old age of the workers and for those incapacitated by injury.

For the abatement of poverty.

To the toilers of America and to those who by organized effort are seeking to lift the crushing burdens of the poor, and to reduce the hardships and uphold the dignity of labor, this council sends the greeting of human brotherhood and the pledge of sympathy and of help in a cause which belongs to all who follow Christ.

Note
1. pcusa.org/acswp/socialcreed.htm

Appendix B

A Social Creed for the 21st Century[1]

We Churches of the United States have a message of hope for a fearful time. Just as the churches responded to the harshness of early 20th Century industrialization with a prophetic "Social Creed" in 1908, so in our era of globalization we offer a vision of a society that shares more and consumes less, seeks compassion over suspicion and equality over domination, and finds security in joined hands rather than massed arms. Inspired by Isaiah's vision of a "peaceable kingdom," we honor the dignity of every person and the intrinsic value of every creature, and pray and work for the day when none "labor in vain or bear children for calamity" (Isaiah 65:23). We do so as disciples of the One who came "that all may have life, and have it abundantly" (John 10:10), and stand in solidarity with Christians and with all who strive for justice around the globe.

In faith, responding to our Creator, we celebrate the full humanity of each woman, man, and child, all created in the divine image as individuals of infinite worth, by working for:

- Full civil, political and economic rights for women and men of all races.
- Abolition of forced labor, human trafficking, and the exploitation of children.
- Employment for all, at a family-sustaining living wage, with equal pay for comparable work.
- The rights of workers to organize, and to share in workplace decisions and productivity growth.
- Protection from dangerous working conditions, with time and benefits to enable full family life.
- A system of criminal rehabilitation, based on restorative justice and an end to the death penalty.

In the love incarnate in Jesus, despite the world's sufferings and evils, we honor the deep connections within our human family and seek to awaken a new spirit of community, by working for:

- Abatement of hunger and poverty, and enactment of policies benefiting the most vulnerable.
- High quality public education for all and universal, affordable and accessible healthcare.
- An effective program of social security during sickness, disability and old age.
- Tax and budget policies that reduce disparities between rich and poor, strengthen democracy, and provide greater opportunity for everyone within the common good.
- Just immigration policies that protect family unity, safeguard workers' rights, require employer accountability, and foster international cooperation.
- Sustainable communities marked by affordable housing, access to good jobs, and public safety.
- Public service as a high vocation, with real limits on the power of private interests in politics.

In hope sustained by the Holy Spirit, we pledge to be peacemakers in the world and stewards of God's good creation, by working for:

- Adoption of simpler lifestyles for those who have enough; grace over greed in economic life.
- Access for all to clean air and water and healthy food, through wise care of land and technology.
- Sustainable use of earth's resources, promoting alternative energy sources and public transportation with binding covenants to reduce global warming and protect populations most affected.
- Equitable global trade and aid that protects local economies, cultures and livelihoods.
- Peacemaking through multilateral diplomacy rather than unilateral force, the abolition of torture, and a strengthening of the United Nations and the rule of international law.
- Nuclear disarmament and redirection of military spending to more peaceful and productive uses.

- Cooperation and dialogue for peace and environmental justice among the world's religions.

We—individual Christians and churches—commit ourselves to a culture of peace and freedom that embraces non-violence, nurtures character, treasures the environment, and builds community, rooted in a spirituality of inner growth with outward action. We make this commitment together—as members of Christ's body, led by the one Spirit—trusting in the God who makes all things new.

Note

1. Approved by the General Assemblies of the National Council of Churches (November 7, 2007) and Presbyterian Church (U.S.A.) (June 27, 2008); pcusa.org/acswp/pdf/socialcreedreceivedbynccc.pdf